LIFEBOAT HEROES

The news that there was a ship in danger was immediately flashed to lifeboat stations along the coast.

It was a night ripe for disaster. Tumultuous waves were raging around the coasts of Britain. Battling through them were fishing vessels, cargo ships and oil tankers. All were being subjected to a severe battering from the angry sea.

Amongst them was a Danish coaster named the *Lady Kamilla* which pitched and rolled through the sea.

Around the coasts at their shore stations, the lifeboatmen drew their oilskins and sou'westers about them as they stared at the waves lashing themselves upon the rocks. In the central operations room of the Royal National Life-Boat Institution in Poole, Dorset, the night duty officer stirred in his bed. He slept lightly, ready to awaken when the telex or telephone alarm rang shrilly to summon him to cope with trouble on the seas.

Suddenly, this trouble came. Something tragic happened to the *Lady Kamilla.* No one knew the cause of the trouble. But the crew was called to action stations and the radio operator was ordered to send out an SOS message for help.

The RNLI duty officer read this on his telex. "Danish coaster *Lady Kamilla* in distress 15 to 20 miles west of Trevose Head." It had been relayed from the Coastguard at Land's End, and it also informed the officer that lifeboats from Padstow and St. Ives had gone to pick up the *Kamilla's* survivors.

Immediately, the control room officer sprang into action. He summoned other RNLI officers to assist him, and began spreading out his charts to pinpoint the site of the *Kamilla's* disaster.

Messages were sent to other lifeboat stations telling the crews there of the *Kamilla's* plight. The Clovelly lifeboat was among those which joined in the search. The sea proved to be a tough oppponent for this vessel. But a worse sufferer was the St. Ives lifeboat, whose cockpit was swamped by a huge wave which put most of its electronic equipment out of action.

Reports that flares had been

4

Thousands of men owe their lives to the gallant heroes of the Royal National Life-Boat Institution.

seen to the west of its station prompted the Kilmore Quay lifeboat in Ireland to be launched, to join the search for the *Lady Kamilla.* Nothing was found, but the crew's bravery was to have a high price. While the craft was returning to its station, huge waves capsized it twice. On both occasions the craft righted itself. But one of the waves carried away a lifeboatman. After the lifeboat had reached the shore, another crew took it out again to search for the missing man. And an Irish Army helicopter added its crew's eyes to the task. But all this brought no result, for the lifeboatman was never recovered.

On this busy Christmas Eve morning in 1977, the lifeboat service was having a busy time. Seven lifeboats were looking for the *Lady Kamilla.* They were not successful and the ship was presumed to have sunk. A liferaft was found containing two survivors, the rest of the crew of nine were thought to have drowned.

One lifeboat was sailing near a Panamanian vessel which had gone aground off the East Coast. Another had gone to assist a coaster which was in trouble off South Wales. Both of these vessels reached shore safely.

Fortunately, this was not a typical night for the lifeboat service. Most nights are less eventful for this organisation, which is always on duty around the coast of Britain and Ireland.

Founded in 1824, the RNLI is a registered charity and all of its income comes from voluntary contributions, leaving it free of government control. Its early lifeboats were propelled by oars and sails until, in 1890, the first steam-powered lifeboat went into service. Experiments with petrol engines started in 1904 and with diesels in 1932. All lifeboats now have twin diesel engines.

With the exception of the wars of 1914-18 and 1939-45, lifeboats have been launched between 300 and 500 times a year during most of the Institution's history. But this figure has now risen to nearly 3,000 a year with over 1,000 people saved from death and hundreds more taken off vessels, brought medical aid or otherwise assisted.

The 200 stations operate over 250 offshore lifeboats fitted with radio, radar, radio direction-finding equipment and echo sounders. In addition, some have automatic navigational systems and some are also provided with auto-pilots.

One of the newest classes of life-

boat is the *Solent,* whose hull is made of moulded wood and contains 24 watertight compartments. There is enough plastic foam built into the boat to keep it afloat, even if all the watertight spaces are holed. And if it is capsized, the boat rights itself.

This lifeboat was put to the test when a French trawler, *L'Espérance,* ran on to some rocks off Guernsey. Sea conditions were bad and the wind was building up to gale force. It set out from St. Peter Port and headed for the trawler which had heeled over on some rocks. The trawler's crew of four had escaped from their ship in a liferaft.

Seeing these men bobbing in the sea in their raft, the lifeboat launched a rubber dinghy carried on its decks. With this, the lifeboat crew rescued the men in their liferaft and took them safely aboard to the lifeboat.

Finally, the Frenchmen stepped ashore from the *Solent* soaked to the skin and clinging to the few things they had managed to save before abandoning their ship. They were four more people among the many who owe their lives to the skill and bravery of the men who constitute Britain's great lifeboat service.

THE OLD MAN OF THE FOREST

At first sight a potto hanging from a tree deep in the heart of the African forest looks like the nest of a bird that has used fur as its building material.

About the size of a squirrel and with a short, stumpy tail, the potto is reddish-brown in colour with a dark stripe down its back.

Its enormous eyes are each surrounded by a black ring. This rather gives it the appearance of a very learned old man.

The potto has almost human-like hands and feet, except that there are only three complete fingers besides the thumb. The first or index finger is only a stump.

Pottos are nocturnal animals: that is, they sleep throughout the day. When night falls they set off on their slow and methodical hunting expeditions from tree to tree.

IN SEARCH OF FOOD

With its sharp teeth the potto gnaws a hole through the bark and wood of a tree. Then it inserts its long slender middle finger to drag out insects and grubs. It also eats fruit, leaves and birds' eggs.

While on these hunting expeditions, the potto is just as happy walking upside down under a branch as on top of it. It is very slow and deliberate in all its movements, often stopping and apparently thinking what its next move should be.

Africans say that the potto takes such a long time to make up its mind that it can starve to death just travelling from one tree to another.

The fable probably arose because the potto is naturally very thin. Its backbone and shoulders sticking up through its fur certainly give it the appearance of being nothing but skin and bone.

Pottos are found in all the forest lands from Ghana to the mountains of Kenya. In many districts they are held in great veneration by the tribesmen, who believe that the little animal's enormous eyes weep tears that are a cure for all sorts of ailments. Witch

The potto often seems to stop and think about its next move in the jungle. It stops so often, in fact, that Africans say it can starve to death just travelling from one tree to another!

doctors do a thriving trade selling small bottles of "potto tears." The "tears" are just water.

A close relative of the potto is the awantibo (sometimes spelt angwantibo). It is smaller, of lighter build, has no tail, and its ears are bigger. The fur is yellowish-brown on the back and a lighter shade underneath, and it is easily distinguished from the potto by the white line down its nose.

Awantibos are native only to the forests bordering the Old Calabar River of Nigeria. Even there it is very rare and it is seldom seen in zoos.

Both the potto and the awantibo belong to the same group of animals as the better-known bush baby.

THE HARD LIFE OF THE MAYANS

Among the thick jungles of Mexico, the Mayan peasant farmers built wonderful cities. They worked on them each year when the harvest was over and they had few tools to help them, so it was hard, slow work. First they had to clear a patch of ground, cutting down the trees and jungle plants with their stone axes. Then the building stone had to be cut from the quarries and shaped with picks and chisels made of stone. They also had bone picks and bone drills for boring holes, but they never had any metal tools. They never learned to use wheels, as the people of Europe did, so they had no carts. They had to carry everything they needed themselves. The big blocks of stone were rolled along on logs to the building site, but as the Mayans had never learned to use animals as beasts of burden, they had to haul the stones themselves. For handling sand and mortar, they used shovels and spoons made of wood, or of turtle and oyster shells. All the time, expert masons and architects watched to see that everything was done properly.

Thousands of years ago, the world was much colder than it is now. Parts of the land were covered with glaciers and big sheets of ice, just as the South Pole is today.

As so much of the water had turned to ice, the seas were much shallower, so that North America and Siberia were probably joined together by a narrow strip of land.

The men of these times lived by hunting and fishing. They followed the herds of wild animals wherever they went and probably some of them crossed from Siberia to North America, across the bridge of land, in search of mammoth, bison and other animals.

Then, slowly, the weather grew warmer. The big ice sheets melted, so the water in the seas rose, and the bridge of land disappeared. America was cut off from Europe and Asia.

These hunters, the early American Indians, gradually moved South. Some of them reached the areas we now call Mexico and Peru.

Some of the people who settled in Mexico became known as Mayans. At first they settled down to farming, but as time went on they learned about building, and they built themselves some big and wonderful cities.

A Mayan farmer had a very hard life. Before he could plant seeds he had to clear a patch of ground from thick jungle, and had only a stick, which was sharpened to a point and hardened in the fire, to dig holes for the seed-planting which followed.

The ordinary people of the ancient Mayan empire in South America did not live in the fine cities they had built, only the priests and nobles lived there, but on festival days everybody gathered in front of the temples to pray. Then there was a gay time for all, with music and singing and dancing. The Mayans made music by beating drums and turtle shells and blowing flutes and whistles. Conch shells were used as trumpets. Dancers had jingling bells tied to their wrists and ankles. The dances were colourful and noisy, for the people wore their finest clothes. They had capes and head-dresses made from the feathers of brightly-coloured birds and they wore feather bracelets around their legs and arms.

In spite of this he grew all kinds of things which the farmers of Europe had never heard of. There was a kind of corn called maize, and there were also red and black beans, tomatoes, melons, potatoes and pineapples.

At night the farmer went home to his little hut on the edge of the jungle clearing. It was made of sticks and mud, thatched over with straw.

There the Mayan women had been busy all day, grinding corn, cooking, and weaving straw and tree fibres into baskets used for carrying food, and matting for beds.

When the harvest was over, there was no rest for the farmer. The Mayan people were ruled by priests, and the priests made them build cities and great temples, where the statues of their gods could be placed and sacrifices made to them, so that the crops would grow well.

9

HOLD TIGHT!

With a roar from its gas burners, the hot-air balloon rose into the air. It was the start of a flight which an Americn balloonist, William R. Berry, will never forget.

As the balloon began to gain height, Berry thought he heard a distant shout. But he was so engrossed in his instruments, that he took little notice.

At just over 900 metres, he reached up and shut off the burners. In the silence that followed, he heard a small voice calling, "Please mister, won't you get me down?"

Berry looked over the side of his basket and froze with horror at the sight of a boy dangling from a rope below. Hanging helplessly in space was eleven-year-old Danny Nowell of Mill Valley, California. He had somehow got his hand tangled up in one of the ground handling lines attached to the balloon's basket and had been dragged into the air.

Unable to reach the boy, Berry spoke quietly to calm him, and pulled on the line which would open the valve to release the balloon's hot air and bring it down gently.

Just over 3 km from the point where his hair-raising flight began in 1963, Danny came back to earth with a bump, frightened but unharmed.

He had been an unwilling participant in one of the races which have become a part of the sport of ballooning, which has seen a great revival in recent years.

THE NEVER-ENDING SEARCH FOR OIL

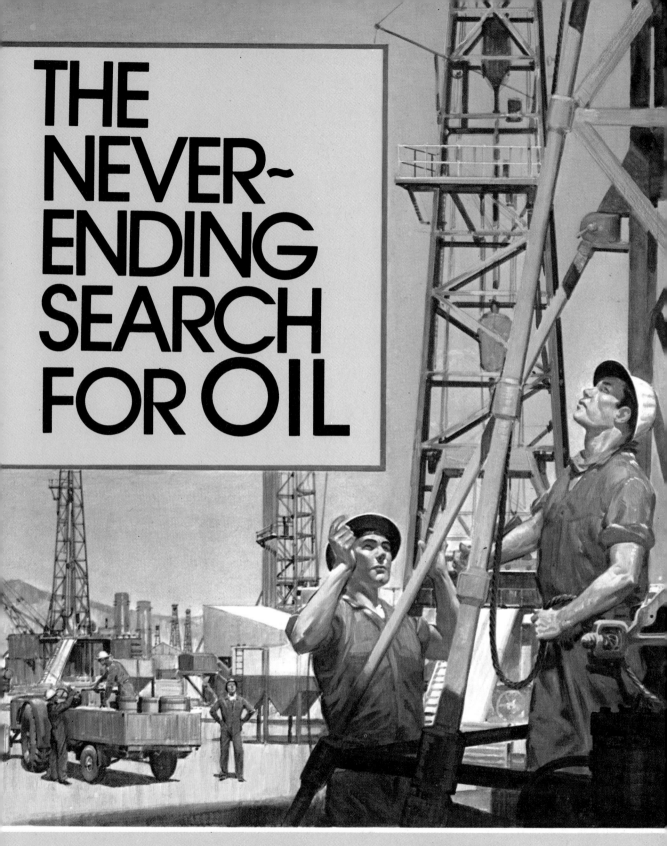

Far below the waters of the North Sea, and deep beneath the sands of the desert in some of the Arab countries, lies a substance which is the lifeblood of the Western world. This is oil, which fuels virtually every branch of industry from transport to electricity generation and from heating to aviation. It is made into petrol, aviation fuel, diesel oil and kerosene as well as a vast number of by-products that range from chemicals to proteins.

Today, we could not do without it. Yet it is hard to realise that the oil industry is just over a hundred years old and that it gained its momentum from the demand for fuel that followed the industrial revolution.

Even before mineral oil was discovered, whales were being slaughtered indiscriminately so that their large quantities of blubber could be boiled to produce animal oil.

Across the Atlantic in Pennsylvania, engineers drilling for brine found large amounts of oil coming to the surface. This was bottled and sold as medicine. Before long, however, three men, Colonel Edwin Drake, George Bissell and Benjamin Stillman, realised the big industrial possibilities of oil and formed the first company to search for it. In August 1859 they started to drill, and within weeks the well had reached a depth of 21 metres and crude oil began bubbling to the surface. The news spread round the world and, almost like the Klondike gold rush, people from all nations joined the search in the hope of making their fortunes with this liquid gold.

Oil revolutionised modern transport and, because of its discovery, the internal combustion engine was invented, and with it came the motor-car and the aeroplane. A thicker grade of oil was produced and the diesel engine was evolved. Kerosene (or paraffin) is used for heating and, in contrast, powers the fastest modern jets.

Today oil and natural gas between them provide more than half the world's total energy needs. Modern industrial countries are already spending huge amounts in trying to develop other sources of power, because of the colossal rise in oil prices. But no matter how much money they spend, it will take many years for them to find alternative supplies. New nuclear power stations can take up to eight years to build, and to sink a new coal-mine may take almost as long.

When oil was discovered in Pennsylvania, it was more by luck than judgment. Fortune-seekers who came afterwards began drilling and found nothing, and it was soon realised that much more information about the world beneath the surface of the Earth had to be obtained.

Needed by the Industrial West to operate its machinery, to run its industry and heat its buildings, oil has brought good wages to those who drill for it and wealth to the sheiks in whose land it is found.

Some of the first oilfields were found in the simplest way—by seeing oil seeping through the earth, or floating on the top of a river. Although some kinds of oil can be obtained from plants, bodies of dead animals and fish, the majority of it comes from deep beneath the ground. This mineral oil is called petroleum, from "petra" meaning rock and "oleum" meaning oil. Petroleum, however, includes not only the liquid oil as it comes from the ground (crude oil), but also natural gas—found sometimes with oil and sometimes by itself.

Usually, oil is discovered in the most inaccessible places—under deserts, under the sea and under the ice. Even today, geologists can never be certain where oil will be found, for there is still a certain element of chance in its discovery. Most oil has to be drilled for, and there is only a fraction of the earth's surface beneath which it exists. The men and materials needed for a drilling operation can cost many millions of pounds. Mistakes can cost a fortune.

Because of the enormous areas of territory to be explored, aircraft equipped with special cameras flying at a predetermined height and speed on a pre-determined path take a series of overlapping photographs. The oil prospector is looking for various clues which these photographs can reveal, not only geological features, but details like soil patterns and the paths of streams, which will indicate where oil-fields are likely to be.

Today, with the help of satellites fitted with computers and electronic and television equipment, a detailed map of what is underneath the earth can be plotted, and the geologists with their skill and past experience can, by looking carefully at all the evidence that the pictures reveal, select the most likely areas for sinking a well. The next stage is to visit these areas to study the terrain at first hand and take samples of the soil, rocks and vegetation. If all the signs are favourable, the experts then recommend places for drilling.

Although continuous research has been going on since the first oil well was drilled over a hundred years ago, nobody can be quite certain how oil was formed, but it is thought that the gas that comes from oil may be more than one hundred million years old.

Let us take an imaginary journey back millions of years and try to imagine what was happening in the shallow seas all those ages ago. In the seas were innumerable billions of minute creatures which, when they died, fell to the bottom of the sea and sank into the mud. There they became mixed up with dead sea plants and pieces of freshwater plants carried down to the seas by rivers. More mud and sand, which the rivers brought to the sea, buried these creatures and plants deeper and deeper in the sea bed, but before they could decay they were trapped in a layer of mud.

Gradually, as time went on, the weight of the sea and the mud squeezed this mixture into something harder and beds or layers of rock were formed.

All this time, the creatures and plants imprisoned down below were slowly turning into oil—a change that took millions of years to complete.

In the Middle Ages, when very few people could read, news was spread by word of mouth. Pedlars, minstrels, and other travellers were always sure of a welcome because of the news they brought to towns and villages. Gossips spread local news on market days, and rules and regulations were announced by town criers. Important national events, like the proclamation of a new king, or a declaration of war, were announced by heralds in each country town.

Kings and statesmen were sent news from abroad in letters from ambassadors. From Elizabeth I's reign, spies were sent abroad as well for collecting information. News of impending invasion, like the sighting of the Armada, was spread by lighting beacons (left). In the 16th century hand-written weekly newsletters were sent by "intelligencers" to patrons for a fee; later, printed "Courants" were sent out, containing only foreign news. Anyone daring to print home news was prosecuted. Prynne in Charles I's day was pilloried (right), imprisoned, fined and deprived of his ears for his seditious comments on affairs.

Journalists exchanged news in Old St. Pauls near Fleet Street. In the Civil War both sides produced rival tracts; then, at the Restoration, Court and official news appeared in the London Gazette, which still exists today. The first "daily" came out in 1702. This Daily Courant was keenly read in the popular coffee houses of the day, though the rich had copies delivered. Newspapers were heavily taxed and editors were often bribed by politicians to print slanted news.

Many famous writers have been journalists, including Defoe, Swift, Lamb and Dickens, who is seen above reporting debates in Parliament in shorthand. Not till his time was this allowed. By 1785 London had eight morning papers and nine evening papers, including the Daily Universal Register which in 1788 became The Times. During the Napoleonic Wars it sent out the first war correspondents.

18th century stage and mail coaches spread news faster. News of battles was often shouted out by the coaches' guards, then spread quickly by word of mouth. Meanwhile, papers circulated round the country within two days, thanks to the coaches. W. H. Smith founded his famous firm in 1792, and specialised in distributing newspapers fast. In the next century his son used the new railways and started a chain of railway bookstalls. On the streets newsmen blew their horns (right) to draw attention to their wares. Placards in their hatbands showed which paper they were selling.

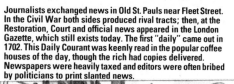

NEWS...

Left: Although Parliamentary reform was in the air in the early 19th century, attempts to bring out cheap papers for working men ended in governments stepping up newspaper taxes. Those who dared write against the government were imprisoned if the papers had not paid stamp tax, and so were the printers. But illegal papers still came out. In the 1850s and 60s all taxes were abolished to allow working men to read reputable papers. The Daily Telegraph appeared in 1855. It sold more copies than The Times, but the latter remained the most influential paper in the country; in fact, it was already world-famous.

The 19th century produced daring and adventurous journalists, including W. H. Russell of The Times, who exposed the follies of the High Command in the Crimean War, and the sufferings of the troops. In 1871 Henry Labouchère sent messages out of besieged Paris by balloon. During the Boer War young Winston Churchill reported for the Morning News.

Today we take it for granted that we know what is happening anywhere in the world within hours, but before the invention of the telegraph in 1837 news travelled slowly. Reporters used pigeons to convey racing and boxing results. Until the Channel cable was laid in 1850, The Times kept a cross-Channel steamer ready to bring news from Europe. By telegraph, when it was fully developed, news could travel across the world in a matter of seconds. The Transatlantic cable was laid in 1866.

Railways were delivering papers faster, and from 1840 the penny post carried them to even more outlying places. Reading habits changed. Men who had walked or ridden to work now wanted papers to read on trains and buses. In 1886 an American watchmaker named Mergenthaler invented a linotype machine which set type quickly. Rotary presses printed papers faster and paper itself became cheaper because less expensive wood pulp was used. This resulted in the coming of the ½d. newspaper which brought the newspaper habit within everyone's reach.

Alfred Harmsworth, later Lord Northcliffe, who had already produced bright, cheap magazines, bought the Evening News in 1894, then started the first ½d. "Daily," the Daily Mail, in 1896. The Daily Mirror followed at the same price in 1903. "All the news at half the price" was his slogan. Eye-catching articles and competitions brightened the papers, and his writers had to use simple, direct language, new in journalism. The Daily Mail spread his ideas, but he did not try to influence The Times or the Observer, which he also bought.

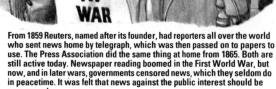

From 1859 Reuters, named after its founder, had reporters all over the world who sent news home by telegraph, which was then passed on to papers to use. The Press Association did the same thing at home from 1865. Both are still active today. Newspaper reading boomed in the First World War, but now, and in later wars, governments censored news, which they seldom do in peacetime. It was felt that news against the public interest should be suppressed.

Illustrated journalism really began with the Illustrated London News in 1842. At the time artists were employed to make pen and ink drawings, but by the end of the century, photography was starting to be used for the newspapers. In 1904, pictures were first sent by wire. By 1896, the Coronation of Tsar Nicholas of Russia could be filmed, and in 1907 Charles Pathé had the idea of filming the week's news for showing in cinemas everywhere.

By 1922 the first news broadcasts were heard in Britain, wireless having come into being earlier in the century. At first it was ruled that only news that had already appeared in the papers could be used, so that radio would not compete with the news agencies. News broadcasts of those days were taken from agency reports and listeners were told that each bulletin was the agency copyright.

In 1926, the General Strike began with newspaper stoppages. During the strike The Times managed to produce a single sheet distributed by hand, and the Government had an anti-strike paper edited by Winston Churchill. It was at this time that radio news came into its own. Restrictions on fresh news were dropped and the nation depended on the radio. It was in 1926 that the B.B.C. was formed; from then on radio news-spreading grew apace.

In the 1930s popular papers often thought up new stunts to increase circulation, but when the Second World War began in 1939, papers got smaller because of the paper shortage and people relied more and more on the radio, including the people of occupied Europe and the Resistance Fighters. Today, TV cameramen follow the troops into action, just as film cameramen did in the Second World War.

Left: A new development in papers came with the introduction of the colour supplement, a well-illustrated magazine given away with the newspaper. This carries advertisements which help pay for it, as well as news features. Nowadays the latest and freshest news usually comes to us by TV or radio, but television news has to be as factual and unbiassed as possible, so we usually turn to our papers for more detail, comment, opinion and background information. Some people respond to the spoken word: there is room in our lives for both kinds of news media.

Thanks to satellites in space acting as relay stations, we can see events on the other side of the world as they happen. The pictures are beamed at the satellite and bounced down again to avoid being lost by the curve of the earth. There is a saying that bad news travels fast. It is certainly true to say that these days ALL news, good or bad, travels fast. The coming of television has led to news and pictures of events, which have taken place on the other side of the world, reaching our homes within a very short period of time. New technology in communications is being developed all the time and this will speed up the process of bringing us the news even more.

THE GREEDY INTRUDER

One of Britain's best-known summer visitors is the cuckoo. This bird arrives from its winter quarters in tropical and southern Africa sometime in April.

It has a bad reputation which is certainly well-deserved. Too lazy to build a nest and to bring up its young, the cuckoo victimises small birds such as reed warblers, hedge sparrows and robins, by removing an egg from their nests and replacing it with one of her own. When it hatches the young cuckoo is very sensitive to touch and will kick and jerk if the rightful occupants of the nest touch it. One by one, the young nestlings are kicked out of their home until only the cuckoo is left. In this way the gluttonous baby receives all the food that would have been given to the other birds. This makes it grow at an alarming rate, but it still clamours for food from its unfortunate foster parents, even after it has left the nest.

The cuckoo is unique among British birds in another way because the adults start the migration journey back to their winter quarters in Africa in late July or early August, some weeks before their youngsters are ready to fly.

It remains a mystery how these young birds, completely neglected by their real parents and therefore having no contact with them at all, are able to make the long and difficult journey to Africa over sea and land entirely unaided.

MEET THE MAN THEY CALL 'MR. HELICOPTER'

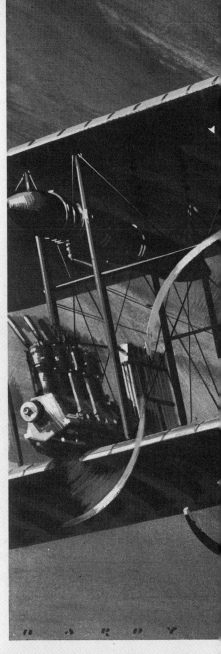

Igor Ivanovich Sikorsky was born on 25th May, 1889, in the Russian city of Kiev. As a child he was deeply interested in science, engineering and astronomy, as well as the fantasies of Jules Verne and the ideas of Leonardo da Vinci.

At the age of 12, foreshadowing his great achievement, he built a rubber-powered helicopter model which lifted itself into the air. But much aviation history was to be made before he would fly in a real helicopter of his own design.

As he grew, the idea of flying still filled his thoughts. In 1903, when he entered the St. Petersburg Naval Academy, the world was buzzing with the news of powered flight by the Wright brothers in faraway America. But not until 1908, when he went back to Kiev for engineering studies, did Igor read proper accounts of Wilbur Wright's demonstration flights in Europe. The accurate reports and pictures determined him to make aviation his career—and to build helicopters.

Sikorsky begged his family to lend him money so that he could go to Paris, then the centre of flying in Europe, and buy aero engines. He got his wish and soon, in that great city, he was meeting famous men like Henri Farman and Louis Blériot, soon to fly the English Channel.

SLIGHT LIFT – OFF

When he returned home, Sikorsky took with him two Anzani engines, which he built into two helicopters. Clattering, shaking and smoking, these contraptions each showed enough "lift" to raise themselves slightly off the ground, but they would do no more.

The designer decided to try his hand at conventional aircraft instead and built a small hangar in a field outside Kiev. With a few enthusiastic helpers, he set to work, allotting each design an "S" for Sikorsky and a number. His offspring met with varied fortunes. S-1 refused to fly; S-2 *did* fly across the field many times, but came to grief in a ravine on a more ambi-

Sikorsky's S-6 biplane, which flew late in 1911. The improved S-6-A made its inventor's name in Russian aviation, and began his greatness.

tious trial. The next plane, S-3, flew, but ended in a frozen pond.

With all these experiments, the young designer was learning his trade. S-5 was a good machine which stayed airborne, sometimes for more than an hour; and S-6, rebuilt after many experiments as S-6-A, could take Sikorsky and two passengers. In 1912, it won first prize at the Moscow Aircraft Exhibition, and an offer of the post of chief designer from the Russian Baltic Company. This concern made railway rolling stock and had just opened an aircraft division.

At the age of 23, Igor Sikorsky was high in the budding world of aviation. His first design for the company, the S-6-B, won a gruelling contest against all comers, beating Farman and Nieuport designs into second and third places.

Crew fight to extinguish an engine fire, while Sikorsky turns back to land. The fact that the engines could be reached in flight saved the lives of the crew on more than one occasion. The Ilia Mourometz II became a heavy bomber flying against the Germans in the 1914-18 war.

The first raid took place in February 1915, and from then on Sikorsky was chief designer, test pilot and instructor of military crews for the bombers. In September 1915, one was shot down by German fighters. Sikorsky re-designed the tail to accommodate a rear gunner (right), after which no more bombers were lost to fighters.

Next, he turned to another dream, long in his mind—a four-engined aircraft! As the machine took shape, it was named *Grand*, from the French word for "big". This was a fitting name for its 28 metres wing span and its long, tall cabin with large windows. At a time when few people flew, and when they did were muffled up in goggles and furs in the icy blast of an open cockpit, the *Grand* offered flying luxury. It had plush seats, a sofa, table, toilet and clothes' cupboard inside the warmth of a spacious cabin. The pilots were in the forward part of the cabin. Ahead of them, if anyone wished to brave the wind, was an open viewing balcony.

After the *Grand* had flown for the first time on 13th May, 1913, its fame spread far and wide, and even the emperor, Czar Nicholas II, came to inspect it in person and talk to its designer.

Next came the mighty and justly famous Ilia Mourometz design, named after a legendary Russian hero. The second aircraft was flown by Sikorsky and a tough crew, from St. Petersburg to Kiev. He and his colleagues were still learning about designing and flying aeroplanes.

ENGINE ON FIRE

This journey brought them through blinding cloud with only crude instruments, an engine fire in the air and a fatal near spin, all of which were overcome.

On the last part of the flight, Sikorsky handed over the controls and climbed out on to the walkway he had built on top of the rear fuselage. Standing in the open, blasted by the slipstream, he gripped the safety wire with freezing fingers and stared down at a blinding white sea of cloud tops, a sight which remained etched in his memory.

Beginning in 1915, the Russian Air Arm flew squadrons of the big Ilia Mourometz design as heavy bombers agianst Germany. But in Russia, the whole fabric of society was crumbling into chaos. Sikorsky began to see that his own aviation dreams would crumble with it. All that he had worked so hard to achieve would be destroyed in the roaring tide of revolution.

He did not want to leave Russia, but he *had* to build and fly aeroplanes. He would have to find a new country and start all over again.

In February 1918, Sikorsky boarded a steamer at the Russian port of Murmansk and, leaving behind the ashes of a brilliant career, he set out to find new opportunities to design, build and fly aeroplanes.

Passing through Newcastle and London, he went to Paris where he obtained a commission to design a heavy bomber for the French Air Service.

Throughout the summer, in a hotel room, he worked on the design. It was approved and five planes were ordered. Then, in

The S-29-A, the first aircraft built by Sikorsky in America, was very successful after a shaky first test flight. It flew on to a long and profitable career.

November 1918, came the armistice and big bombers were not needed. The order was cancelled and Sikorsky was high and dry again. Deciding to try his luck in America he took a boat to New York.

The situation was no better there. On both sides of the Atlantic aviation was at its lowest ebb, with orders cancelled and war surplus planes and engines being sold for rock bottom prices. The American Air Service, impressed by his record and experience, gave Sikorsky a brief design study contract. But when it was finished he was again out in the cold.

To pay for board and lodging he lectured on mathematics, astronomy and aviation, living for most of the time on bread and baked beans.

He knew that in such a huge country there must be a rebirth of the aviation industry soon. Encouraged by the help and meagre money of his fellow Russian immigrants, Sikorsky launched the Sikorsky Aero Engineering Corporation on a shoestring on March 5, 1923, at a time when big aviation companies were going broke. The company began business on a farm near Roosevelt, Long Island, New York, and, with materials bought in small batches or from junkyards, the S-29-A twin-engined biplane took shape.

It was built out of doors in the farmyard, and when it was ready for flight it was towed to Roosevelt Field (the airfield from which, later, Lindbergh and other New York to Paris pilots were to take off).

POWERFUL ENGINES

The S-29-A's war surplus engines did not give their expected power, and Sikorsky made a forced landing on the first flight. More money was painfully but doggedly scraped together, the plane was repaired and strengthened, and with new and more powerful engines, it flew on to a long and profitable career.

The Sikorsky sun was rising again through hard work, skill and persistence. Work went on, on landplanes and flying boats.

In September 1926, the S-35, a superb streamlined tri-motor biplane, was ready for flight. It was to be used by Captain René Fonck, the famous and bumptious First World War French air ace, in his attempt to win the $25,000 prize offered by Raymond Orteig for the first non-stop flight from New York to Paris.

The S-35 performed excellently, but against Sikorsky's wishes it was readied for the flight too quickly. Loaded down with fuel, it failed to take off, crashed and was destroyed in flames. Fonck and his co-pilot escaped but the other two crewmen did not.

Sikorsky's work continued. The twin-engined S-37 monoplane flew to South America across the Andes and beyond. The S-38 amphibian was built in large numbers, and besides use by military services, flew on pioneering air routes and exploration. Charles Lindbergh, as consultant to Pan American Airways, flew one on an airmail service to Panama and this began a long working friendship with Igor Sikorsky.

They collaborated on design points of the ten big S-40 amphibians being built for Pan American, and flew one on many of the type's long distance runs. The S-40s were reliable and tough. None ever crashed.

The next big flying boats were the S-42 "Flying Clippers" which were far ahead of their time in performance and design. They took a long list of aviation records.

For some time, Sikorsky's firm had been (and still is) part of the United Aircraft Corporation and the last of the big flying boars were built at Stratford, Connecticut, in a factory shared with the Vought company.

The VS-44A "Flying Aces" boats —three were built—were used throughout the Second World War as V.I.P. transports on long distance trans-ocean flights. VS, by the way, are the initials of Vought and Sikorsky.

Left: In the spring of 1931, the giant Sikorsky S-40 amphibian made its first flight from the waters of Long Island Sound.

Above: The highly efficient S-42 "Flying Clippers" flew out across the Atlantic and Pacific, pioneering air routes. They were built by Sikorsky. Below: Three VS-44A "Flying Aces" flying boats were built. They flew non-stop transatlantic services during the Second World War, carrying V.I.P. passengers in great comfort.

But despite the excellence of its big planes the Sikorsky company made no profit on them. In 1928, the heads of the parent United Aircraft Corporation decided reluctantly that Sikorsky must be closed down. For the second time in his life, the Russian pioneer faced an eclipse of his work. But he was read for the situation.

He had never forgotten his first interest in aviation—the helicopter—and he had quietly carried on a study of its problems. He left the meeting at which he was supposed to be put out of business with the promise of enough money to build and test a helicopter.

In 1910, Igor Sikorsky had abandoned his attempts to build a helicopter after his second design had scurried and clattered across his parents' garden in Kiev, barely able to lift its own weight.

Years passed before he built his third helicopter. It was, on 14th September, 1939, strapped into the pilot's seat on a skeletal framework, that he eased back the pitch control of his third helicopter, the VS-300. Its whirring blades lifted him off the ground. The 75 hp engine roared and vibrated. The whole machine shook. But it hovered happily a few inches off the ground, tethered by strong cables in case it proved too eager to fly.

HOVER POWER

For years before, Sikorsky had been able to see all the advantages of the helicopter's ability to take off and land vertically, to operate in confined spaces and to hover over one spot under full control.

Its possibilities as a rescue and transport vehicle, a "flying crane," were very clear to him.

All he had to do was to build one that would work and learn to fly it . . . and then show it to the world.

The VS-300 went through many changes of rotor layout and even flew with floats from water. Time and time again, Sikorsky demonstrated its powers. On one occasion, he had it hovering over the same spot for more than an hour and a half. The little helicopter, much loved by its creators, finished its career in October 1943, when it went to the Ford Museum at Dearborn, Michigan.

The first production helicopter was the R-4, which flew with many air forces and rescue organisations. The first recorded mission of mercy by a helicopter was a flight in bad weather on 3rd January, 1944.

It was made by a U.S. Coastguard R-4 to deliver desperately needed blood plasma to injured crewmen on a U.S. Navy destroyer. The first use of the now familiar rescue sling was also on an R-4 mission.

This was to pluck two men off a sinking barge on 29th November, 1945.

Since those days, thousands upon thousands of lives have been saved in peace and war.

The other tasks that only helicopters can perform would fill a book. In peace, they lift people from the sea, from the jungle, from cliffs and mountain tops, from flood and fire. They can carry almost anything anywhere and put it down gently with great precision. They service oil and gas rigs far out at sea.

MAID OF ALL WORK

In war, they drop troops and weapons right where they are needed.

They fly into murderous fire to lift out injured men or downed pilots, they lower their listening sonar "ears" into the sea to find submarines and carry weapons to deal with them.

They hover near the flight decks of aircraft carriers as "plane-guards" to pick up the crews of planes which crash.

After his retirement as engineering manager of Sikorsky Aircraft on 23rd May, 1957, at the age of 68, Igor Sikorsky continued as consultant, lending his vast experience to the designers of today's big helicopters.

In his long and brilliant career, more than 100 awards have been bestowed on him in half a dozen countries. All these were accepted with characteristic grace and humility.

The legendary lone transatlantic pilot, Charles Lindbergh, a close friend of Sikorsky, once said of him, "As a man, not just an aviation pioneer, he's one of the greats of his time."

A moment in history. For the first time Sikorsky eases the VS-300 off the ground. The date to remember was 14th September, 1939.

More helicopter history. It is 29th November, 1945, and two men are winched to safety in the now well-known rescue sling from a wrecked barge by the U.S. Coastguard Sikorsky R-4.

Some Sikorsky helicopters chosen at random from the thousands which work all over the world.

1. S-61N all-weather helicopter airliner of British European Airways operating between Penzance, Cornwall, and the Scilly Isles with a crew of three and 25 to 28 passengers.
2. One of two HH-3E ''Jolly Green Giant'' rescue helicopters which flew from New York to Paris in 1967 to complete the first non-stop helicopter crossing of the Atlantic.
3. A Westland-Sikorsky Whirlwind H.A.R. 10 rescue helicopter of R.A.F. Strike Command.
4. S-67 Blackhawk, designed as a high-speed ground attacker, which holds speed records at 220.8 m.p.h.
5. S-64 Skycrane, which, as its name suggests, is a ''flying crane'', able to lift a ten-ton load.
6. CH-53 assult cargo helicopter looping the loop.

THE TALE OF A TINKER

John Bunyan's book 'Pilgrim's Progress' has been circulated more widely than any other book save the Bible.

Three hundred years ago a boy was born into a humble country family living in the small Bedfordshire village of Elstow. He was given the name of John. From his earliest days he was a grave, contented child. As he grew older and stronger, he spent his days mending the local farmers' tools, repairing pots and pans, and learning the trade of an itinerant tinker like his father. His family was extremely poor, but he was happy, and enjoyed nothing better than to accompany his father on the roads.

Too poor to own books, he would listen to the stories of the grown-ups. Each evening John's mother would light the little rush-light and settle down by the fireside. Night was the time for stories. Outside the cottage door lurked a still, menacing landscape of empty lanes and ominous trees.

His mother was the family teller of tales. John knew all of these tales of fiends and hobgoblins, and strange beasts that lay in wait for unsuspecting travellers, and they never failed to thrill him.

By the age of 16, John Bunyan had become one of the most popular figures in the village. He enjoyed dancing with the local girls with whom he was a great favourite, and ringing the bells of the parish church each Sunday. But times were changing, and before long England was plunged into that most bitter form of fighting, civil war.

The nagging grievances of Parliament against its King, Charles I, found expression in the fiery denunciations of Oliver Cromwell, who had placed himself at the head of the Parliamentary forces. Young as he was, John was inspired by grand thoughts of righting ancient wrongs. Much against his parents' wishes, he went off to fight on the side of Parliament against the King.

During the Civil War he had many exciting adventures, narrowly escaping death on several occasions. Once he was very nearly drowned when crossing a river. But the incident that deeply disturbed him involved an attack upon a Royalist town. This was to be particularly dangerous and several of his company were picked to take part. John was to be one of them. A friend of his pleaded with him to be allowed to go in his place and John reluctantly agreed. Later he learned that his friend had been killed shortly afterwards by a musket ball. This deeply affected John, who felt that he had escaped death by a miracle.

After four years of bitter fighting, the Royalist cause was destroyed. In January, 1649, King Charles I was executed and John returned to his native Elstow. He had seen enough of fighting to last him for the rest of his life. Aged little more than 20 years,

When his friend who took his place died in battle, Bunyan felt he had been saved by a miracle.

he married a woman as miserably poor as himself. Without money or household goods, she nevertheless brought with her two books which had once belonged to her father.

Books were rare and expensive in those days, and John and his wife together slowly read them over and over again. The religious nature of the books had a strange effect on John's over-imaginative and superstitious mind. He began to regard many of his harmless pleasures as sinful, and he began to neglect his old companions. No longer did he go dancing on the village green on holidays. He even stopped ringing the church bells. He thought that by giving up a greater part of his old life he would find inner contentment and peace of mind.

One summer afternoon, while walking along a lane, he came across a group of village women sitting together in the sun. Because he was feeling lonely he stopped to listen to their conversation. To his great surprise, John discovered that these simple peasant women had found for themselves a bright new religious world.

He saw in a flash just what was wrong with his life. He asked them to what church they belonged and was told they were all members of a small chapel, or meeting-house. Before starting to walk back to his cottage he agreed to attend their meetings.

The leader of the chapel was a man called John Gifford, who offered to help John study the Bible. John worked hard and, in time, he decided he wanted to try his hand at preaching the word of God. He became a deacon of the chapel, and regularly preached before the country folk who crowded the wooden benches. He was a persuasive talker and made what he had to say easy to understand. At last John had discovered the inner contentment he had been seeking.

SECRET WORSHIP

Great changes were taking place in England. The Government passed from the hands of a cheerless Parliament, and King Charles II ascended the throne. Under a new law, all meeting-houses belonging to the Nonconformist sects were closed. Worship, therefore, became a matter of secrecy. The Nonconformists met together in woods, fields and barns. But Government spies were everywhere, and many preachers were dragged from their hiding places and thrown into prison. In spite of the danger, John continued to preach. Disguised as a poor carter he went from barn to barn, helping the suffering Nonconformists to stand true to their faith.

One day, while preaching in a farmhouse, John was arrested and thrown into prison. Brought to trial, his judges reminded him that his trade was tinkering and not preaching. But he remained defiant in the face of possible banishment and death. "If you let me out today, I will preach again tomorrow, by the help of God."

He lay in prison for 12 years, although he could have been released if he had promised not to preach any more. From prison he had to support his wife and four children by making shoelaces.

Although he could not preach, he could write. During his long imprisonment, he wrote a religious autobiography, *Grace Abounding*, and *Pilgrim's Progress*, which has been described as the greatest religious book ever written.

After years of imprisonment, John Bunyan was released. He went back to his little Baptist Chapel at Bedford and spent the remaining years until his death in 1688 preaching and helping others.

Many millions of years ago, a vast sea stretched from the Mediterranean region to what is now central Asia. Where once its eastern waters lay, there is now an arid, empty basin—the Gobi Desert. It extends over 1,600 kilometres from east to west, straddling the border between Outer and Inner Mongolia, at the very heart of the continent.

The Mongolian word *gobi* is the name given to the flat-bottomed depressions that abound in the area. In fact the desert is made up of a series of "gobis", separated in some places by rolling, stony ridges, and in others by lines of flat-topped rock hills.

The surface of the Gobi is nowhere much less than 900 metres above sea level. But the land on every side, except the east, rises high above it to give it its basin form. Southward lie the heights of Tibet, and in the west is the great Altai range, whose spurs extend deep into the desert itself.

Through the ages many changes have occurred in the Gobi region. There have been periods when the climate was damper and more kindly than it is now. Fossilised dinosaur eggs have been unearthed, and evidence has been found that the mastodon and the giant rhinoceros flourished there, too. Later the region was the home of Stone Age Man.

Today, as for thousands of years past, much of the Gobi is uninhabitable. The Chinese call it Shamo, the "Sand Desert". In fact sand and dunes such as those seen, for example, in the Sahara, are rare in the Gobi. There are extensive areas of bare rock, since the fierce winds have carried away the sand or soil that once covered it. Elsewhere the surface is generally of pebbles or gravel.

Many of the little stones are brightly coloured, and they include types that we should regard as semi-precious. A Mongolian guide, seeing a European traveller gathering some of these, was highly amused at this interest in "ordinary pebbles."

Over much of the desert there is no vegetation. Here and there a hardy tree called the saksaul survives by thrusting its thick roots down to the moisture that exists underground. In the hollows and around the rare waterholes, typical desert growths are seen—sparse, tufted grass, and sometimes dwarf willows and tamarisks. The bottoms of the hollows are often filled with salt bogs.

Some watercourses run into the Gobi from north and south; but as often as not they are dry, and when water does flow in them it is soon lost by evaporation, or by seepage into the thirsty ground.

On the northern fringe of the desert, where the land rises towards the Mongolian Plateau, the conditions are those of semi-desert. Here there is more rain, and grass is more plentiful, providing pasture for herds of sheep, goats, cattle and the two-humped Bactrian camels.

In the Gobi, as in Africa and Arabia, the camel is the traditional means of desert travel and transport. Though probably introduced from the west, it has become so naturalised that it is even found living wild, as are the sturdy horses of the region.

The desert sees little rain, but the Gobi plays a big part in bringing rain to other regions. The high temperature of the air above it in summer sets up a centre of low pressure which draws in air. This is a major cause of the south-east monsoon that carries rain into China and south-east Asia in the summer months. Sheltered by mountains, the Gobi itself receives little of this rain.

In spite of its forbidding character, the Gobi has long been important as a route westward between the mountains, linking China with the West. Through the region ran the great Silk Road, along which this valuable commodity was carried from China to the Mediterranean in the Middle Ages. Marco Polo, the famous Venetian traveller, visited the desert in the late 13th century. Seven hundred years later, tales of

THE DESERT THAT LOST ITS SAND

his coming still survive among the older Mongolian tribesmen.

The southern rim of the desert is now part of the Chinese Republic of Inner Mongolia. Most of the rest belongs to Outer Mongolia. The latter is an independent state, but is largely under the influence of its Soviet neighbours.

Traditionally the Mongolians have either led a nomadic existence, wandering with their camels and herds from pasture to pasture, or have settled in small communities, living in little round houses called *yurts,* made of camel-wool felt, stretched over wooden frameworks.

Most now find themselves organised into Communist "collectives", sharing their herds under official direction. Some, however, have chosen to retain their old way of life. They live mainly on the products of their goats and sheep, sometimes supplementing their diet with the game they can shoot on the more fertile margins of the desert. Antelope and gazelle, partridge and pheasant, are among the wildlife to be found.

Camel caravans can still be seen making their way over the old routes, toiling on from well to well. But their days are numbered. A railway now crosses the desert, joining the Trans-Siberian line to the Chinese network in the south-east. Close to the railway, in the south-eastern desert, there are other signs of a new age in the Gobi—a flourishing oilfield, and a busy airport. Along the ancient camel trails, motor vehicles now raise choking clouds of red dust.

In winter the Gobi is transformed. The colours of the rocks and stones are often cloaked in snow—and the temperature falls dramatically.

With modern fuels and modern means of transport, the world of the Gobi is changing rapidly, and the lives of its sturdy inhabitants are being made easier. But it is to be hoped that the beauty and fascination of this unique desert land will not vanish altogether.

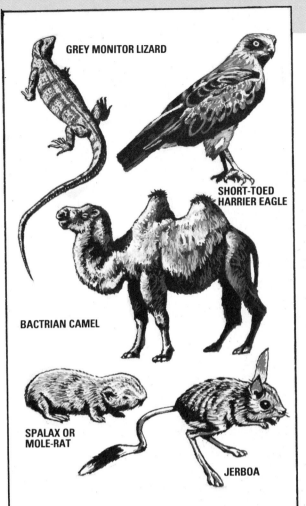

GREY MONITOR LIZARD

SHORT-TOED HARRIER EAGLE

BACTRIAN CAMEL

SPALAX OR MOLE-RAT

JERBOA

Pictured here are some of the creatures that somehow manage to survive in the Gobi Desert.

Mongolian horsemen catching a wild horse. In the background can be seen the tribesmen's portable tent-houses known as yurts.

FOR YOUR PLEASURE

Since very early times people have liked to be amused and entertained, perhaps with music or dancing, play-acting or maybe clever acrobatic feats, whatever happened best to suit their mood at the time. But those ancient folk did not have the medium of television or radio, theatre or cinema, as we do today. Instead they relied upon the skills of the strolling player or street entertainer.

Often these entertainers were called "wanderers" because, as the name suggests, they wandered from place to place. They lived on whatever they could earn from the ever-changing audiences of fairs, markets, hangings, and indeed any public place where there was most likely to be found a good gathering of people.

It would be difficult to say when the first strolling entertainers and musicians were seen. It is certain that they existed in England long before the Norman Conquest, and the old Anglo-Saxons used to call them "gleemen." The "gleemen" travelled around in troupes which would often include whole families, very much like the circus acts that we can still see today, where whole families take part. There would be jugglers, tumblers*, conjurers, play-actors, musicians and singers, and keepers of performing animals such as bears, monkeys, dogs, hares, and even pigs!

Street entertainers of this kind were also to be found in many of the ancient civilizations, in Greece, Italy, Egypt, as well as many of the Eastern countries. The Greeks were well used to watching skilled rope walkers and enjoyed the

*another word for clowns

28

antics of clever acrobats, jugglers and tumblers. Homer, the famous Greek poet, mentions in particular the remarkable skills of the tumblers, who danced as well on their heads and hands as on their feet.

By the Middle Ages the streets of England were thronging with many kinds of entertainers. There were the walking preachers, fortune tellers, posture masters*, stilt walkers, many more musicians, and a marked increase in the number of performing animals. The cries of the entertainer mingled with those of the street crier, so that the narrow streets were both noisy and crowded, and often dangerous.

CRUEL TRAINING

Many of the performing animals were savage, especially the dancing bears. This is thought to be the result of extreme cruelty in early training. The bears were made to stand for long hours on heated iron plates, so automatically the animal would lift its feet up and down to prevent burning, and all the time a drum was played. After constant repetition the bear would then only have to hear the drum and it would begin to raise its feet and appear to dance.

Similar methods were employed to persuade monkeys, dogs, hares, and other animals to jump through hoops and to walk tightropes. Punishment it seemed was the only way for the early trainer to achieve the desired results from his animals. Happily, today we have much more humane methods; gentleness and great patience are exercised in

*another name for contortionists

order to first gain the animal's confidence.

Other dangers were the vagrants, beggars, pickpockets, card-sharps and fake fortune tellers, all of whom posed as entertainers, tricking honest folk into parting with their money and thus giving the true entertainer a bad name. By the 16th century these vagrants had become a really serious problem, their ranks having been considerably swelled by soldiers who had returned from the wars, many of whom could find no work and so turned their skills to theft and deception.

Queen Elizabeth introduced vagrancy laws, imposing severe penalties upon all street entertainers who practised their profession without first obtaining a licence from at least two justices of the peace.

Victorian London enjoyed the delights of the "Fire kings" or the "Salamanders" as they were sometimes called. These gentlemen swallowed fire, produced by lighting sulphur and inhaled and eaten whilst still alight. "Tow* eaters", and "sealing wax eaters" competed just as vigorously for fame, a dangerous profession and one that often resulted in severe stomach burns.

A much pleasanter pastime was that of "The Chinese Shades". This may well have been the forerunner of the Magic Lantern. Many owners of "Punch and Judy" booths would take to the "Shades" in the winter months. A piece of white calico was stretched across the front of the little stage to serve as a screen whilst one or two candles glowed at the back to cast shadows on the screen. It required two men to work the show, one to play accompanying music

*coarse and broken part of flax or hemp

and to speak the parts of the small wooden characters, and the other to move the small figures about with lifelike movements. Not really unlike puppets or marionettes.

In the 19th and early 20th centuries many foreign entertainers could be seen in England. There were Italian organ grinders with performing monkeys and a host of Italian musicians and singers, as well as German bands and many double acts, such as a "Whistling Man and Dancing Boy", or singers harmonising together. Another interesting artist who frequented the streets was the popular "Likeness Cutter", who would cut from either black card or paper a clever likeness of anyone who cared to sit for him.

The Great War in 1914 brought an end to many of these entertainments, especially those of the Italian and German artists. A few still carried on but gradually street entertainers became quite rare. However, the unemployment of the 1920s and early 30s brought about a revival and once more there were musicians and street entertainers. Choirs from the mining districts travelled about the country, groups of violinists and solo singers became frequent sights. Often the songs were tragic and rather drawn out, not unlike the old Victorian ballads.

Pavement artists drew with great skill on the pavements of most large cities. They used coloured chalks and would leave an empty cap beside them hoping for a few coppers from the passing crowds. Many of their pictures would be scenes of great battles, because of course many of them were war veterans themselves.

Today we still have a few street entertainers left but they are becoming increasingly rare. We still hear from time to time of an "escapologist" who will attract large crowds to watch him either escape from a sealed box thrown into a deep river, or free himself from the bonds of complicated chains or ropes in a matter of moments. And there is still the "human cannon ball" or the "amazing tightrope walker" who can perform seemingly impossible feats.

Occasionally "buskers" will be seen entertaining theatre queues. Most of them will be musicians playing

The music of the organ grinder could be heard in the streets of towns all over Britain during the 19th and early part of the 20th century.

perhaps an accordion or violin, but now and then we might hear the odd solo singer. "Buskers" is an old word that was once applied to travelling pedlars and ballad singers who entertained people in the taverns and coffee houses.

In recent years a festival was held in Winchester which centred around different street entertainers such as clowns and musicians. It was an attempt to bring back an interest in these folk, and indeed it would be a pity if they vanished altogether from our streets.

The crowd which gathered about the street entertainer would provide easy pickings for the pickpocket who would take to his heels once his crimes had been discovered. Below: with coloured chalks the pavement artists created a variety of scenes which captured the imagination of the passing crowds.

A Thief In Search Of The Sun

Watching the Malayan sun bear happily snoozing in the warmth of the Asian sun, one finds it a little difficult to imagine that this gentle-looking creature spends much of its time as a wicked thief.

The very sight of a bee's nest is enough to bring out the sun bear's criminal tendencies, because it can never control its insatiable greed for honey.

Whenever it comes across a nest of bees, it shakes off its usual lazy habit of catching prey with the least amount of effort and, bounding with energy, pounces on the nest and rips it apart with its large curved claws. Then with its long curling tongue it begins to lick the honey and relishes its delicious taste. The infuriated bees buzz frantically round the gluttonous robber of their nest in an effort to sting it so that the sun bear will leave their food alone. But their stings cannot penetrate the bear's thick protective coat of black coarse hair, so it continues to taste the delights of its favourite meal. Nothing, it seems, could possibly stop it from doing that! Even when the sun bear has eaten an enormous quantity of honey, it cannot resist trying to reach the grubs that lie in awkward, inaccessible holes at the back of the nest. By curving its long tongue, the sun bear even manages to reach those too.

When the sun bear is not busy raiding the nests of bees, ants and termites, it spends a lot of time climbing up trees on its bandy legs in search of a warm and comfortable place to rest. It is found in the Malay Peninsula, on the islands of Sumatra, Java and Borneo, and in Burma.

At home in the dark dense jungles of these Asian countries, the sun bear can be seen performing the comical and amusing antics which make it such a popular animal at zoos. It can easily be tamed if it is caught at a young age. It is often captured by two men who come into the jungle clearing with nets and ropes. Once the sun bear is caught, it is placed in a large basket and carried off to a town where it will be sold as a pet. However, as it grows older, the sun bear can become very bad-tempered, and sometimes even dangerous.

The peculiar name given to this strange little robber is said to have come from the yellow crescent on its chest, which is supposed to represent the rising sun, but it could just as easily have come from the animal's love of basking drowsily in the warmth of the sun's rays!

About mid-day on 16th October, 1793, a rough cart rumbled slowly over the filthy cobbles of the Paris streets. On all sides jeering, yelling faces grimaced up at its sole occupant. On the straw-covered floor of the cart sat a woman in a ragged white dress, with her hands bound, yet with brief traces of majesty in her bearing and of beauty in her haggard face. Although not yet forty years of age, her hair had gone completely white. She seemed not to see the clawing fingers of the leering crowds or hear the obscene shouts as the cart rattled on its way.

At the Place de la Révolution the cart was brought to a halt. The woman mounted the scaffold and laid her head beneath the blade of the guillotine. Such was the end of an emperor's daughter, once the most beautiful and pleasure-loving princess in Europe.

Marie Antoinette, fourth daughter of Maria Theresa of Austria and Francis I, was born in Vienna on 2nd November, 1755. She spent her early years in a dazzling court surrounded by lovely things and interesting and gifted people. One day the seven-year-old Mozart, who was giving a piano recital at the palace, slipped on the polished floor and was picked up by Marie Antoinette. He smiled up at her gratefully, "You are very kind; when I grow up, I shall marry you." But such a thing could never be, outside a fairy story. The brilliantly-gifted Mozart went to an early pauper's grave and Marie Antoinette was married at the age of 15 to Louis XVI of France, then heir to the throne.

Louis was a kind man but awkward and timid. He often wished, even before the Revolution, that he had been born a commoner. But not so Marie Antoinette. She loved being a queen.

When Louis became King in 1774, Marie Antoinette upset a great many people by trying to further the interests of her native Austria. She also angered a group of statesmen by her extravagant and reckless ways. Undeniably beautiful, she glittered and laughed her days away while most of France lay tortured by miserable poverty and cruel landlords. In the minds of a great many people, she became the symbol of the yawning gulf that lay between the aristocracy and the general public.

It was obvious that very urgent reforms were needed in France, but Marie Antoinette forced the easy-going Louis to resist any real attempts at change. She was not at all concerned with the struggle for survival among the peasants in the countryside or towns. When told that people were too poor to buy bread for their starving families, she replied indifferently, "Then let them eat cake."

So long as Louis entrusted the

For years the ordinary people of France had been seething with discontent. On 14th July, 1789, they stormed the hated Bastille prison in Paris. For Louis XVI and his beautiful queen, Marie Antoinette, it was . . .

THE END OF AN ERA

finances of his kingdom to statesmen like Turgot and Necker, a Swiss banker, he managed to divert real trouble. But he was too easily swayed by greedy courtiers, who saw in Necker a direct threat to their social positions and salaries and their lives of idle, luxurious ease. Under this strong pressure Necker was dismissed.

From that moment onwards things went from bad to worse. Louis was forced in 1789 to call the States-General, the members of which demanded greater powers, and finally declared themselves a National Assembly. At the beginning Louis was quite content to work closely with the new Assembly, but Marie Antoinette's influence proved much too strong. He broke all the promises he had made and decided to seek aid from Austria against the Revolution which was threatening to split France in two. Even then, he did not seem to realise that Marie Antoinette, rather then he, was blamed for the conditions in France. Had he listened less to her and more to his councillors, the situation might have been saved.

On 14th July, 1789, the huge prison-fortress of the Bastille in Paris was captured by the people, its fall heralding the end of the old régime in France. The mob stormed the defences, shouting their new motto "Liberty, Equality and Fraternity," and released the prisoners. The day of

reckoning for the royal family was close at hand.

The King and Queen tried to flee from Paris in 1791. But an old soldier recognized the King from his picture on banknotes, and passed the information on to the appropriate authorities. The coach was stopped at Varennes and, under heavy escort, brought back to Paris. His attempt to leave the capital convinced the whole of France that the King, influenced by his frivolous wife, was inviting invasion from other countries.

This conviction grew rapidly: stories, many of them hideously distorted, spread through the streets, taverns and market places of France. Finally, in August 1792, the floodgates of public opinion burst open. Charges were brought against Marie Antoinette of treachery in the war with Austria. A violent mob broke into the Tuileries Palace, seized the royal family and imprisoned them in the Temple. From there King Louis was led in December to stand trial, and in January 1793 to execution.

Queen Marie Antoinette was now on her own. Everywhere mobs howled against the "Austrian woman" as they called her. She must have guessed that her days were numbered.

The aristocrats were dragged by their former workers from their looted châteaux to swell the long queues to the guillotine. Those who managed to escape were fortunate; others were hounded mercilessly and captured at check-points and ports. France, in the throes of a dreadful madness, had reached the point of no return. Informers, professional people, small-time officials, shopkeepers and humble seamstresses found to their horror that the Revolution, far from bringing about better conditions, was turning in upon itself like some mad, blood-crazed beast.

Everyone went in daily fear of suspicion and arrest. It was only a matter of time before the Queen would die before a howling Paris mob.

In August, 1793, Marie Antoinette was taken to the prison of the Conciergerie, where common criminals and murderers were confined. Here her young son, known as King Louis XVII although he never reigned and his exact fate is unknown, was taken from her. Screaming with anguish, she pleaded with her jailers to allow the boy to remain. They laughed in her face. As a final act of cruelty, they taught the boy to use foul, obscene language and forced his mother to listen.

At her two-day trial she bore herself with great dignity and patience. But the trial was a travesty of justice. With the insults of the crowd dinning in her ears, Queen Marie Antoinette was convicted of treason and condemned to an untimely death.

The Getty Museum. Below: Raphael's "Holy Family", painted about 1509, hangs in the museum.

THE ROMAN VILLA THAT HOUSES A FORTUNE

Marble portrait of a Roman, dated about A.D. 220.

Carved Roman pot, with serpent handles.

"I thought it would be worthwhile to create one building in the Roman tradition," wrote oil multimillionaire J. Paul Getty in 1974, two years before he died, in his late Seventies.

The site he chose was just off the Pacific Coast Highway overlooking the ocean at Malibu, Southern California, and the breathtaking, sun-warmed building he created there gives us a marvellous insight into what a great Roman home must have looked like in ancient times.

Getty, an avid collector of ancient objects and paintings, wanted a permanent home for his collection to serve his memory—a museum whose building itself would reflect the grandeur of his pièces. A lover of Europe and all things European—he lived in England for many years—he settled on Southern California for the site because America was his birthplace and California had the climate which was most like sunny Italy.

Paul Getty had been an art collector since the 1930s. He had special interest in three areas—Greek and Roman antiquities, Renaissance and Baroque paintings, and French eighteenth-century decorative arts. At first he put his collection in a large Spanish-style house at Malibu, but as the collection grew the need for a new museum became urgent.

In his time regarded as the richest man in the world, Getty frequently lamented the destruction that man and the passage of time had wrought upon the buildings of ancient Rome. Could he bring one of them back to life again? He decided to use as his inspiration the Villa dei Papyri at Herculaneum.

Herculaneum was Pompeii's twin town and, like Pompeii, was overrun with molten lava when Vesuvius erupted in A.D. 79. It was perhaps the "smarter" end of Pompeii, where the richer people had their seaside homes. In fact,

even the volcano's eruption was kinder to it, for the fact that it was angled slightly away from the main slope of Vesuvius led to it receiving a slightly less destructive lava flow.

As a result of that, in those parts of Herculaneum which are uncovered today, some of the buildings are in an even better state of preservation than those of Pompeii, and notably the original Roman woodwork in the houses is in excellent condition.

There was a good deal of information available on the Villa dei Papyri for Getty's builders, and it was clearly one of the most beautiful homes in Herculaneum.

From the first or second century B.C. until the catastrophe in A.D. 79, the original villa was occupied by wealthy Romans of the patrician, or noble, class. The site of lava-covered Herculaneum was only discovered in the eighteenth century when monks, digging a well, struck the marble seats of the town's ancient theatre.

Later, interest in excavating the region grew, but the interest was not to discover the villas in all their glory but to find any treasure that had been left behind by the stricken occupants. For this reason, the excavators dug downwards and then tunnelled horizontally.

A Swiss engineer who supervised the digging and tunnelling into the Villa dei Papyri made plans of it. But after about 18 years of this work, interest evaporated. The tunnels gradually caved in and the villa remained covered up. It is still covered up today, and indeed the Swiss engineer's plans proved to be the major basis for Getty's Malibu reconstruction.

The museum gardens include the same types of trees, flowers, shrubs and herbs which might have been growing two thousand years ago in the Villa dei Papyri. The bronze statues in the gardens are modern casts of the ones found during the eighteenth-century excavations of the villa; the originals are on display in the Naples Museum. Illusionistic wall paintings along the garden walls recall original frescoes found in Pompeii and Herculaneum.

The original villa lay on a gentle slope within sight and sound of the sea. Its main residence was built around a court, or peristyle, and there was another court to one side of it. Deep open corridors surrounded the main court. In the centre of the court was the garden, with a long narrow pool. Garden, pool, corridors, courts and all the inner rooms of the villa are duplicated in the Getty Museum.

What was particularly interesting about the original Herculaneum Villa dei Papyri was that it contained a library of Greek and Roman works written on papyrus rolls—hence its name. Most of the works were philosophical and some were by one Philodemus, who lived in the first century B.C. and who was befriended and patronised by Lucius Calpurnius Piso, the father-in-law of Julius Caesar. One theory is that at one time Piso owned the villa.

Scholars and philosophers didn't always live in the Villa dei Papyri, however. A bust of a Roman author in the library was found to have a line written on it by a graffiti writer of ancient times to the effect that the author's books were very boring.

Just before Vesuvius erupted, burying Pompeii and Herculaneum for so many centuries, the then owner had many of the villa's statues removed, and one of the main rooms, instead of being filled with philosophical texts, was filled with grain.

J. Paul Getty was born in Minneapolis, Minnesota, in 1892 and lived for most of his life in Europe. He established his first museum in 1953; the Villa dei Papyri was opened in January 1974. Getty died two years later, by which time his collection of Greek and Roman sculptures, his paintings, furniture, clocks and carpets had been moved into the gleaming new building.

Only the museum's well-documented guidebook can do justice to all the magnificent treasures the villa-museum contains. Perhaps the best-known piece in the collection, and one for which the owner is said to have had a special feeling, is the Lansdowne Herakles, or Hercules, a statue of the young god-hero with lionskin and club. It is housed in a temple, a small, round, high-domed room, lighted only by a shaft from above.

Although inspired by an earlier Greek work, the Hercules was carved by the court sculptor of the Roman Emperor Hadrian, himself a great art collector and traveller, and was found in his villa at Tivoli, 25 kilometres from Rome. It was later acquired by the Marquess of Lansdowne, and still bears his name.

Almost every aspect of Roman life is reflected in the Getty Museum. It may be a sign of our times that the museum had to be built over an underground car park catering for its visitors (and for which, incidentally, visitors are advised to book their place in advance), but, after you have parked, even as you approach the garage lift, you are welcomed by sixth century A.D. mosaics.

J. Paul Getty believed that a museum should not be a dry, dusty old place, but a fascinating reflection of what it was trying to exhibit—"a statement in itself." He achieved his object with full marks at Malibu in Southern California.

Above: Wall portrait of a lady, early 2nd century A.D.
Right: French bracket clock (1720).

An early Italian Renaissance masterpiece, one of many in the Getty collection.

Right: This pair of wrestlers in the garden of the museum are casts from the originals which were found at Herculaneum. The originals are now in the Naples Museum.

Left: Eighteenth-century French decorative arts were another interest of Getty. This panelled room dates from about 1735. The room originally stood in the Hotel Herlaut on the Place Vendôme, Paris.

SPOT THE CARNIVORE

Two out of three of the creatures shown on this page are rodents. And we wouldn't be surprised if you picked the wrong two! The Black Rat (below, left) is an obvious choice—but how many of you know that the Red Squirrel is the other? The Polecat (below, right), which *is* a carnivore, looks more like a rodent than the squirrel. Actually, the word rodent comes from the Latin "rodere" meaning "to chew," but we tend to associate it with rats and other pests.

The Red Squirrel, unlike the Grey Squirrel, is not a pest. It lives in wooded areas in England and Wales, and, as it is extremely shy, it is not often seen. It lives in a "drey," which is a round nest high in a tree. It eats nuts, acorns, toadstools and mushrooms. The young are born in the Spring of each year, and grow to a length of 20 centimetres, with a tail nearly as long.

The Polecat (right), once found in abundance in Britain, especially in Scotland and the Lake District, is considered to be extinct now in most regions. There are none at all in Ireland, and Wales appears to be the only area where they may be found. They live by rivers and feed on small creatures such as mice, shrews and birds.

The reason you would be unlikely to see the Black Rat (right) in Great Britain is that, on the whole, it prefers a warmer climate. Another name for it is the Ship Rat, because it came to Europe from its native Asia on foreign cargo ships. It was at one time the most common rat in Britain but now it can only be found in the larger seaports. The Brown Rat is often mistaken for the Black Rat as very few people stop to examine a rat's colour!

UNDER THE ARCTIC ICE

Explorers have long welcomed the challenge of the Arctic and Antarctic ice. Men have flown over it, walked and ridden upon it and sailed beneath it. The first man to explore beneath the surface of the thick pack ice of the Arctic region was an Australian, Sir Hubert Wilkins.

He first visited the Antarctic in 1920 with the British Imperial Antarctic Expedition, whose main objective was to reach the South Pole by air. Though the project was dropped, Wilkins was convinced of the value of machines for exploration. In 1922, he spent three months in the White South with the great explorer, Sir Ernest Shackleton. But when Wilkins made his first polar flight four years later, it was over the Arctic.

In 1929, the Wilkins-Hearst Expedition took him back to the Antarctic for a series of exciting, dangerous and valuable flights over unexplored territory. He saw clearly the value of setting up permanent stations for research in the Antarctic. At the time, it would have been impossible to keep such stations supplied by aircraft or surface vessels. Wilkins, consequently, began to think about the use of submarines which could go under the ice.

Wilkins was a man of action. By 1931 he had bought an obsolete submarine from the U.S. navy, modified it for exploration and named it *Nautilus*, after a fictional submarine invented by Jules Verne.

Wilkins took his *Nautilus* out of Spitzbergen on 18th August, 1931, and spent three weeks in the Arctic pack ice to test his own theories.

Later another *Nautilus*, the pioneer U.S. atomic submarine, made her famous voyage under the Arctic ice to cross the Pole on 3rd August, 1958.

THE CITY THAT WAS

Persepolis was one of the great cities of Persia, where the kings of Persia lived from the time of Darius the Great (522-485 B.C.).

Among the most striking of the old palaces and halls was the "hall of a hundred columns". This was on a terrace cut in the rocks and floored with blocks of stone joined together by clamps of iron. Numerous columns supported the ceiling and the total area was reputedly 2½ acres. King Darius is shown here receiving gifts in one of his sumptuous palaces.

It was the custom in the days of King Darius I for the ruler to prepare his own tomb during his lifetime. Darius certainly did this and an inscription on the entrance to his tomb tells of his characteristics and stated that the gods had given him the special qualities of activity and wisdom.

The ruins of his once great palace at Persepolis can still be seen to this day.

THE PRIDE OF PERSIA

MEET THE BRAVE
MEN OF . . .

THE SALVATION NAVY

The name Salvation Navy was bestowed affectionately, and not without due reverence, upon the Air-Sea Rescue Service (ASRS). This Service was inaugurated in 1941, controlled by the Air Ministry Directorate of Aircraft Safety, and jointly co-ordinated by the Admiralty, RNLI and H.M. Coastguard Service.

ASRS launches were manned and ready to put out to sea around the coasts of Britain and in Malta, Gibraltar, and other outposts of British influence. Their express intention was the rescue of any pilot or air-crew member who had baled out over the sea. Crews of sinking ships were also to be assisted.

The men of the ASRS, proudly wearing their badge depicting a high-speed launch in white on a background of Air Force blue, saved hundreds of lives. In their launches, measuring some 19 metres in length, capable of speeds of over 72 kilometres per hour, they showed exceptional gallantry and daring in the face of extreme danger.

BALING OUT

One of the particular concerns of the Service was watchfulness when aerial dog-fights were taking place over the Channel. When a plane was seen to be in difficulties, the men of the launch would keep a sharp look-out for falling crew, and would hasten to the rescue, often reaching the spot where the airman had ditched within minutes of his landing, thus saving another precious life.

As technical advances were made, so more sophisticated equipment became available to the ASRS. Special rescue floats, coloured yellow and red for easy observation and distinction, were moored at strategic points around our coast, notably where aerial fights could be expected to take place. These floats, each about nine metres in length, were there for the use of baled-out fighter pilots. In each float was a change of clothing, some rations, towels, soap and a signalling apparatus for the pilot to contact base, giving his position and float number. From that information, officers of the ASRS checked positions given and made off for the float.

In spite of all this effort, pilots were often missed by searchers. Scientists then developed yellow life-jackets and skull caps for baled-out crews to wear. These were more easily seen by searchers, whether overhead or on the sea.

As soon as a ditched airman had been spotted, the rescue launch would speed to his aid, often within minutes of his landing.

Smoke signals were also developed, orange in colour, which could be seen some 45 kilometres away from the point of release. Fluorescine, used to colour the sea's surface a yellowish-green, also helped pilots of the rescue planes to spot ditched crews.

GENTLE DESCENT

Later developments included the use of motor-powered lifeboats, carried by Halifax bombers and attached to slings fixed to the underside of the fuselage. When released, the lifeboat descended gently, guided by parachutes to which it was coupled. The lifeboats carried equipment which included wireless sets. In May 1943, such a lifeboat was used for the first time, sent to the rescue of a bomber crew which had been spotted in the North Sea, some 100 kilo-

metres from the English coast.

Frequently under fire from the enemy batteries on the coasts of France, Belgium or Holland, and constantly dive-bombed by the planes of the Luftwaffe, the ASRS lost many launches and men. Launches were eventually mounted with guns, but they were difficult to use effectively in the conditions under which they would be required to fire.

A further addition to the Service was the Supermarine Walrus amphibian, which, although scantily armed and having a top speed of only 216 kilometres per hour, did valuable work. It could alight on very rough sea, and could stay afloat in conditions which would swamp most aircraft.

The way in which the ASRS lived up to its official motto, "The Sea Shall Not Have Them", truly earned it the unofficial and affectionate accolade, Salvation Navy.

How would you like to own the history of military uniforms on a set of 50 small cards? Or thrill to the story of "Treasure Island" or study the fascinating subject of military motors! All of these interesting things are shown in coloured pictures on sets of cigarette cards. They were once given away in packets of cigarettes. If Dad, Uncle or Grandad have some, they may give them to you to start your collection.

With one exception, the cards on this page were issued between 1905 and 1938. The odd man out is the cattle rustler, bottom left. He was given away in a packet of tea, as a trade card. Most trade cards cost about 10p to 60p a set. But cigarette cards vary in price from 60p up to £4, depending upon the subject. The best way to keep them is to fasten them in a photograph album, with transparent corners which can be bought for 14p per 500. If you start a collection you can give yourself the name of cartophilist!

IDA LUPINO (PARAMOUNT)

OLD ENGLISH POTTERY AND PORCELAIN.
No. 42. CHELSEA-DERBY

PLAYER'S CIGARETTES
D. G. BRADMAN

The O'Dowd. Book of Snobs.

No. 20 (ARMY CO-OPERATION) SQUADRON, R.A.F.
FACTA NON VERBA

NORTHERN PARTY AT S. MAGNETIC POLE, SHACKLETON'S EXPEDITION.

PLAYER'S CIGARETTES
FIAT "500" CONVERTIBLE SALOON

THE ADMIRAL BENBOW.

ROTTWEILER

LINCOLNSHIRE
AGRICULTURE

WILLS'S CIGARETTES.

PLAYER'S CIGARETTES.
CONSTANCE. THE SORCERER.

WILLS'S CIGARETTES.
A GEYSER.

THE SAINT WHO SLEW THE FIERY DRAGON

"**C**ry — God for Harry! England! and Saint George!" roared Henry V as he led his soldiers through the breached walls of Harfleur, in Shakespeare's history of the king.

Saint George, soldier saint, the martyr and protector of England, is celebrated on 23rd April, Shakespeare's birthday.

The legends of St. George are too numerous to relate in full in one short article. The most fanciful tale claims that he was born in Coventry with a red cross on his chest, and travelled around the land slaying dragons by the dozen. The "official" and more restrained legend is nonetheless colourful and exciting.

St. George was a wandering knight in shining armour from a Christian part of Asia Minor. One day he was passing through the African country of Libya, which at that time was terrorised by a fearsome dragon that dwelt in an evil marsh. The local men had set out to kill the monster, but its breath was so foul and poisonous that they could not come near it. By day and night the great creature roamed the land, killing and destroying with none to stop it.

Then, to keep it contented in its swamp, the people of the nearby city of Sylene each day left two sheep tethered at the water's edge.

The dragon was fed, and so left the unhappy kingdom alone. Then it seems the good people of Sylene ran out of sheep. The dragon felt hungry again and rumbled and roared. In desperation they decided upon human sacrifice to keep the dragon at bay. Each night, lots were drawn and the unlucky citizen was led out to the swamp the next morning and tethered to a stake, to await his or her grisly fate.

Alas, one day, the lot fell to the king's only daughter, Sabra. In vain the monarch appealed for someone to take her place. Not unexpectedly there were no volunteers! So early the next morning, the woebegone Sabra was led out from the city, dressed in the flowing garments of a bride, to meet her death in the dragon's jowls.

FEARLESS

Then, as the fire-breathing creature lumbered towards its breakfast, bold St. George galloped fearlessly to the rescue.

He braved the gnashing fangs and slashing claws, drove his needle-sharp lance through the writhing monster's scaly neck, and pinned it to the soft earth. He then dismounted and freed the grateful maiden. But first he took her girdle, looped it about the creature's neck, and used it like a leash, to lead the wounded monster dog-like towards the city. There was panic.

As St. George walked towards one gate, there was a concerted rush to get out of the other. The king and a few stout-hearts stood firm, for the dragon now seemed quiet and harmless enough. St. George told them that if they all promised to become Christians, he would slay the dragon then and there!

The promise was made, the dragon was slain and twenty-five thousand men, their wives and children, were baptised into the Christian faith. The king offered St. George his daughter's hand in marriage and a huge reward in gold. The soldier saint accepted the former and told the king to distribute the money to the poor and needy.

Sometime afterwards—the date usually given is A.D. 303—the joint Emperors of Rome, Diocletian and Maximianus, began a heavy persecution of Christians in Nicomedia. To save their lives many Christians were giving up their faith, so St. George hastened there to set an example. He strode boldly into the market place and at the top of his voice denounced all the pagan gods as devils. He was promptly arrested by an official named Datianus, strung up, beaten with clubs and tortured with red hot irons. Overnight, he was visited by the Saviour and was miraculously healed. Next a magician was brought to give him poison. It had no effect, except that the magician was so amazed that he turned Christian and was duly martyred for his trouble. Spiked wheels and boiling in lead had little effect on the obstinate saint, who refused to denounce his religion.

Finally, Datianus tried gentle persuasion and was delighted when St. George appeared to agree to enter the pagan temple and offer up a sacrifice. His happiness was short-lived, for St. George fell to his knees and prayed to the Christian God. Fire rained down from Heaven, the walls split and the ground opened and swallowed up the heathen priests and all their pagan idols. For this, Datianus had St. George's head removed by a sword, but was himself struck down by heavenly fire on the way home.

So far, there is nothing in the legend to qualify him as the patron saint of England. He earned this honour almost nine hundred years later when he was reputedly seen helping the English Crusaders fight the Saracen defenders at the siege of Antioch. He was immediately adopted by many knights as their patron, and Richard the Lionheart was supposed to have been thenceforth a great admirer of the saint's prowess.

The truth behind the story is less well-known and harder to find. Some authorities say that there is no basis for the legend at all, and that it is just another case of the Christian religion taking an old pagan story to itself. These experts claim that the legend of St. George is no more than an adaptation of Theseus slaying the Minotaur, or of Hercules killing the nine-headed Hydra in the swamp.

It is almost certain that there was a George, who was martyred at Diospolis (Lydda) in Palestine at about the same date. His venerated relics were still preserved there at the time of the Crusades. He was an officer in the Roman Army, who is reputed to have travelled to Britain. In those days, any Roman soldier who embraced the new religion suffered a very cruel fate. However, when the Church came to compile a book on the acts of the saints and martyrs, he became confused with another George, who came from Cappadocia in Asia Minor and travelled much in Libya. The slaying of the dragon was doubtless written in as a religious allegory, the dragon representing the anti-Christ and the bride in white being the Church.

However, in the 13th century he was given a minor place in the English calendar of saints, and there he remained until 1415, when Archbishop Chichele made his feast on the 23rd April a chief holy day of the year. Pope Benedict XIV (Pope from 1740-58) recognised him as the protector of England, but later, Pope Paul VI struck him out of the list of saints, along with St. Christopher and several others!

HOODED HUNTERS

At speeds of nearly 300 kilometres per hour, the Peregrine Falcon swoops out of the sky at its prey. This handsome bird, so long a favourite with falconers, is found in many parts of the world. It hunts ducks, pigeons and smaller birds, taking them by surprise in the air and striking them to the ground with its needle-sharp talons. Today, very few people practise the ancient art of falconry, but in the Middle Ages it was the most popular sport. Kings and nobles paid falconers to train their own hawks and falcons. When the lord went hunting the hooded birds were carried on a wooden frame called a *cadge*. On open heathland and meadow the hood was removed from a falcon and it was allowed to fly free. Once it had struck down its prey the kill was retrieved and the falcon returned to its master's fist. Sometimes a *lure*, a bunch of feathers resembling a bird, was swung to attract the falcon's attention and make it return.

49

The Wreck Of The FORFARSHIRE

The captain thought he saw the Farne Lighthouse. It was a mistake that doomed his ship to complete destruction.

The story of how Grace Darling and her father rowed out to rescue the survivors of a ship foundering on the treacherous Farne Islands, off the Northumberland coast, is familiar to everybody. But the versions of this disaster always concentrate on the girl's heroism, while details of the actual disaster are usually completely ignored.

On the evening of Wednesday, 5th September, 1838, the *Forfarshire*, an almost new paddle-steamer owned by the Dundee & Hull Steam Packet Co., sailed from Hull down the Humber estuary bound for her home port of Dundee. She carried a crew of 22 men, under Captain John Humble, an experienced coastwise skipper well liked by all. She had a full complement of passengers aboard, and a mixed cargo of hardware, textiles, machinery and boiler-plates. This was a voyage she regularly undertook.

Soon after she cleared Spurn Head and entered open water the wind swung round to nor'-nor'-east and increased considerably in strength. Heavy rain began to fall after sundown. The ship rolled. Many of the passengers, cooped up below deck, were seasick; not a few, travelling for the first time, were frightened. They would have been even more frightened had they known that there was trouble in the engine-room.

The ship had not been many hours at sea before it was found that two of her boilers had sprung a leak. The Chief Engineer urged Captain Humble to return to Hull for repairs. He was brusquely told to increase the pressure in his remaining boilers: the schedule had to be maintained. Back in the engine-room, he found matters had worsened. Water was now flooding out from the two leaking boilers. Since there were fires beneath them, the water-level must be maintained, or they would explode. He had the pumps set in motion; but the water ran out almost as fast as it was pumped in. To make things worse it was so hot that the stokers had to leap clear of it to avoid having their legs scalded. So, the fires went out, and very soon there was not enough to keep the paddle-wheels more than just idly turning. Certainly there was not sufficient way on the ship to counteract the mounting strength of the wind.

Those passengers who dared to poke their heads out on deck and realised this asked what was delaying the ship. Would they be late in reaching Dundee? They were assured that all was well: as soon as the gale lessened, their ship would make up lost time. But the gale persisted. Throughout the whole of Thursday, 6th September, the *Forfarshire* limped along, rolling under the force of the gale hammering her starboard side.

Seasick and frightened, the passengers little knew that worse was to come.

Late that evening the paddle-wheels ceased to turn. Captain Humble ordered the ship's sails to be set, in the hope that he would be able to steer close enough into the eye of the wind to round the dangerous Farne Islands that lay off the coast near Bamburgh. The north-easterly wind had blown him a good deal nearer his lee shore than was safe. With luck, his sails might enable him to head farther out to sea; without that luck, his ship must inevitably be driven nearer to land. Between her present course and the shore lay the Farnes, a notorious hazard to coastal shipping for many centuries past, a ship's graveyard that every seaman feared.

Peering into the gale-filled darkness, the look-out man reported that he could see the flashing of the Farne lighthouse. The captain, assuming that it was the Inner Farne High, nearest to the mainland, ordered his steersman to lay a course to the west of the light. Unwittingly, he had doomed his ship to complete destruction. For it was in fact the Longstone lighthouses that the man had seen, at the eastern end of the rocks and reefs that make up the so-called Farne Islands.

The *Forfarshire* was blown straight towards the dreaded reef known as the Big Harcar, midway between the lighthouse. A great wave lifted her bodily, and then dropped her like a stone on to the reef with a violence that threw everyone to the deck or cabin floor and injured more than a few of them in doing so. The cry, "Abandon Ship!" was heard on all sides, and terrified passengers began stumbling up the companionway. The Second Mate made headlong for the ship's boat slung outboard on the starboard side aft. The First Mate and half a dozen crew members followed him. The boat was launched, and vanished immediately beneath the water.

Stupefied by what had happened, the passengers and other crew members clung to the rails as their ship was alternately lifted and slammed down on to the reef. The fourth time she did so, her back was broken, just abaft the paddle-wheels. The half of the ship that contained the majority of the passengers was swept away like a match-box and sunk without trace. On the other half of the ship the survivors clung frantically to anything that seemed likely to hold firm. The wind howled and the rain lashed furiously down.

The Third Mate took charge. He persuaded the survivors to climb precariously down a rope ladder over the ship's side on to the reef itself, which was now clear of water as the tide was ebbing. There they might have a chance of survival when their ship finally broke up and sank. At first light, now very near, he promised them, they would be seen from the shore, or at least from the Longstone lighthouse, and a rescue attempt would be made. The passengers were by now too stunned to think for themselves, and accepted his advice, taking comfort from what he promised.

The nine wretched men and women clung there, watching their ship disintegrate all about them. Minutes passed, but seemed like hours to them all. It was this pitiful little band of survivors which Grace Darling, the lighthouse-keeper's daughter, saw far away on the reef known as Big Harcar. Thanks to her courage and determination, and the seamanship of her father, the tiny coble they owned was rowed twice across the water between the lighthouse and the reef to rescue the men and women cowering there.

CUTLERY CRAFTSMEN

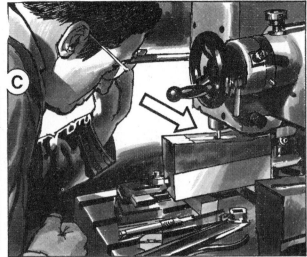

Knives, forks and spoons are such ordinary, every-day articles, that we hardly give them a thought provided they do their job well. However, a great deal of work goes into their design. The designer (A) works closely with sales and production chiefs to produce cutlery which people will like. Endless new shapes and textures or traditional patterns (B) may be discussed and tried. When the final drawings have been approved, the metal-working experts make the master shapes, called tools, from which a small batch of prototypes (C) are pressed. A new design (D) is finally approved and passed for mass production in stainless steel. The factory production line now takes over.

All the master tools for cutting and shaping are fitted to the machines. A powerful machine (E) punches out the shapes two at a time from sheets of stainless steel. The head of the spoon shape is then "cold rolled" twice to iron it down to the correct thickness and cut exactly to size. The spoons are then baked to strengthen them.

A new range of cutlery may include many different items, all of which must be designed to blend together.

At this stage, all the edges of the spoons and forks are rough. To treat this, they are passed to the operators of filing machines which use fast-revolving belts coated with abrasive powders to smooth away the roughness. A special V-shaped belt is used to smooth down the inside edges of the forks' tines. The final abrasive treatment is given with thick discs of calico cloth which give a beautiful finish to the metal. For the final polishing, the cutlery is clamped in rows into a block (H), coated with a special polishing compound and locked into position against a row of revolving calico pads or brushes. For cleaning, the cutlery is packed in metal baskets and immersed for about 60 seconds in each of three sections of the cleaning tank (J) for boiling, shaking and vapour drying in tricol-ethylene.

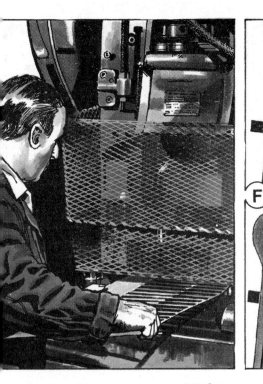

The fork shape has its tines or prongs clipped out on a punching machine. First a double master blade clips out the two outer gaps and a second blade clips out the centre gap. The flat spoons are now ready to receive their half-egg shaping and the forks their curve (F). This shaping is done on a drop stamping machine (G). A skilled operator takes a handful of the flat shapes and, working at great speed to the rhythm of the stamper, feeds them one at a time on to the block (arrowed in white) which is one half of the master shaping mould. The other half drops with great force from above, sliding rapidly up and down on vertical guide rails. If the design features a texture or decoration on the handle (see D), as it does in this case, that is stamped in by a second similar machine. Earlier, while the spoons were still flat, a preliminary polishing was done, because this is easier to do before they are given their curve. But the spoons and forks are still a long way from being finished.

A thorough, detailed inspection is then carried out in which any slight defect causes the piece to be rejected. Approved cutlery is stamped with the maker's name in a small roller machine. If a fine-textured satin finish is wanted, this is made on a further disc-type polisher. The cutlery now passes to the warehouse for yet another inspection, followed by careful packing, either in canteens (K) or in half-dozen packs. It is now ready to be sent to shops or exported. Cutlery craftsmen also create many other beautiful shapes. The four examples above (L), not to scale, are a carving dish, a milk jug, a coffee pot and, on the right, a miniature wine cooler.

British cutlery, made with the perfection shown on these pages, is exported all over the world. The "Made in Sheffield" stamp is the hallmark of quality, backed by skill and painstaking craftsmanship.

The owner of the Boston workshop felt sorry for the half-staved, pale-faced boy who came limping into his office in 1835. The youngster, Elias Howe, wanted to become a mechanic, and he told how he had been set to work on his father's farm when he was six years old. He had hardly received any education, but he was stronger than he looked and he desperately needed to earn money for his family.

After hearing Elias's story, the mechanic, a Mr Davis, agreed to give him a trial. He doubted whether the boy would last the pace for long, but he was too tender-hearted to send him away. As events turned out, Elias proved to have a flair for mechanics. He soon became Mr Davis's chief assistant, and five years later something happened which changed the entire course of his life.

Elias—who was born in Spencer, Massachusetts, in 1819—over-

HE SET THE WORLD SEWING

heard a conversation between his employer and two inventors who had brought in blueprints of a proposed new machine. "A knitting-machine for fishing nets!" Elias heard Davis exclaim irritably. "If you really want to make your fortunes the thing to invent is a woman's sewing-machine. One that will do the work of their hands for them."

From that moment on Elias had only one thing in his mind—to invent a sewing-machine himself!

He told Mr Davis of his intention and resigned from his secure job. For the next few months—while living on his meagre savings—he slaved all day and half the night to try and make his machine workable. Always, however, he ran into an insurmountable snag.

Then one day he had another lucky break. He was walking past a weaver's house when he chanced to look in through an open window. He saw the weaver working at his loom, and noticed how the shuttle moved backwards and forwards, each time making a knot. The shuttle, he realized, was the answer to his problem!

He hurried home and set to work rebuilding his wooden machine. By the winter of 1844 it was almost ready for demonstration—then came disaster. Howe's money finally ran out; he had no way of keeping himself in food, and his father's farm was in even more serious straits than before.

For a time it looked as if he would have to forget all about his invention. At the last minute, however,

To prove just how good his new machne was, Elias Howe arranged a contest with a group of skilled seamstresses—and won by a clear half hour.

an old school friend called George Fisher came to the rescue. He said that Howe could stay as a guest in his house until the sewing-machine had made both their fortunes. The two men went into partnership and the following spring Elias sewed Fisher a suit at the rate of 300 stitches a minute.

Howe's next move was to try to interest the local Boston tailors in installing the machines. But one after another they shook their heads and told him not to waste their time with his "newfangled nonsense." "Why," said one outraged tailor, "if my seamstresses got to hear of such an invention they'd stop working themselves!"

There was now only one thing left for Howe to do—to challenge the seamstresses to a sewing competition. So he hired a hall and arranged to "take on" the city's "five fastest tailoresses." The girls sat at one side the hall with their work in front of them, their fingers eager to commence stitching. On the opposite side was Howe, seated behind his strange-looking shuttle and lock-stitch machine.

At a signal from the jury the competition started. The girls worked more industriously than they had ever done before. But they did not stand a chance against Howe. He finished stitching his article in only seven minutes—almost half an hour before the seamstresses had completed their pieces.

He showed his work to the astounded jurors and they agreed that not only had he won the contest, but his work was much neater and better-finished than that done by hand. It was a triumph for the sewing-machine, but Howe's difficulties were not over yet.

Despite the result of the competition, George Fisher decided to withdraw his support. He had already spent more than a thousand pounds in backing Howe, and when he learnt that each machine would cost approximately £100 to manufacture, he said that he could no longer afford to be Howe's partner.

Back on his own again, the inventor was thrown into despair. He was now married with a baby, and he was forced to return to his father's farm as penniless as the day he had left it. He took a job as an engine-driver, and after vainly attempting to sell the American patent of his machine he sailed to England in 1846 to try his luck there.

In London he found a businessman who paid his £3 a week to use sewing-machines in the making of underwear. But while the businessman grew rich, Howe was again reduced to starvation level. He worked his passage back to America as a ship's cook and again took a job in a Boston engineering workshop.

Soon after this his wife, weakened by months of undernourishment, died. This blow, plus the fact that other inventors were now improving on his machine and putting in into everyday use, almost finished Howe. He felt cheated and without hope; then another friend from the past came to the inventor's aid.

The man, who had been one of the jurors at the famous sewing competition several years earlier, offered to redeem Howe's patent —which was in a pawnbroker's shop in London. With the patent back in his possession, Howe sued the men who had stolen his invention from him.

The law case was a protracted one, and it was not until 1854 that a High Court pronounced that Howe, and no one else, was the true inventor of the sewing-machne. Encouraged by the verdict, the former farmhand built his own factory to produce the machines.

At the time there were few business careers open to unskilled women. But the advent of the sewing-machine changed all that. Girls with no previous talent for stitching were able to work as seamstresses, and the whole face of commercial America was changed.

When Howe died in 1861 he was a rich and honoured man. One of his last acts was to renounce the patent rights on his invention. "I have made enough money from it already," he said. "Now I want the world to benefit from my machine," To this day his wish has been carried out.

BARRELS OF OAK

The noblest of all our native trees is, of course the oak, "English oak" is a term we often use to give high praise—not only to objects made of that timber but to people who have displayed sterling qualities of courage and toughness against great odds. We talk, too, of "heart of oak"—the essence of a noble timber. For centuries our great explorers' vessels, and our men-of-war—ships like Nelson's *Victory*—were built of oak timbers and planking: there was no finer shipwright's timber to be found in all the other forests of the world.

One craft that has always depended on oak, to the exclusion of all other timbers, is that of barrel making (also known as coopering). The barrel maker or cooper is extremely "choosy" in the oak he selects for his product: nothing but the finest will satisfy his demands, and he knows how to judge this, for the handling of oak is a tradition handed down from his forefathers for generations, perhaps for centuries.

If possible, he selects an oak tree that is not less than two hundred years old. He does not need to have it felled in order to count its "rings": he judges the tree's age by a simple, traditional rule-of-thumb method. A two-hundred-year-old oak will be approximately 3 metres in girth—or a good metre in diameter—at breast height. When selected, the tree trunk is cross-cut into lengths according to the size of the barrels to be made with a few spare centimetres to give a working margin and, even more important, to allow for the curvature of each "slave" that goes to make up the barrels.

With "beetle," or "maul," and wedges, he splits the massive block of oak down its "radial lines" into a large number of triangular segments, like massive slices of cake. Then, with his "fromard", assisted by a mallet in the case of a large oak trunk, he splits each of these segments from end to end. Each individual cleft will be parallel with the outside of the segment, from which the bark and sapwood have already been pared. As he presses, or hammers, his fromard he works it deftly to left and right. This results in uniform cleavage down the grain and avoids cutting across the grain, as a saw would certainly do.

Because the segments are triangular, like long prisms, each stave is slightly narrower than the one before it. The outermost staves may be 150 millimetres wide and 25 millimetres or so thick; the innermost ones less than half that thickness and width. They will all be sorted later, according to their proportions, for different sizes of barrel. From a good oak "bole" the cooper will have cleft a hundred or more staves. So far, of course, they are only rough-cleft, ready for the next operation.

Look at any barrel and you will see that all its staves not only curve outwards to the "equator" and then inwards again, to top and bottom, but also vary in width, being narrowest at each end and widest midway along their length. This means that each stave is slightly curved down each side. In addition, each stave is slightly convex outside and correspondingly concave inside. Each stave, therefore, is a masterpiece of precision-shaping by the craftsman. To achieve this remarkble shape he uses an unusual tool, his "jointer".

The jointer is a giant plane-in-reverse: a two metre-long beam of beechwood, anchored to the floor at one end, raised on a trestle at the other, so that it slopes. The plane blade protrudes upwards through its upper surface. The cooper holds his roughly shaped stave, and runs it firmly over the upturned plane blade, giving the stave a slightly rocking, or seesawing, motion as he does so. Working by eye alone, he soon produces a delicate curve along the full length of the stave, slightly bevelled at the same time, to fit its neighbour on either side. When he has "shaped" all the staves he needs he is ready for "raising", or "setting up", the barrel.

The staves are ranged round the barrel bottom (also of oak), held lightly in position by a hoop. Then heat is applied to them, causing them to bend inwards, so that their bevelled sides come closer together. Then a series of hoops are placed round them and slid and hammered upwards and downwards until the staves are so constricted as to be locked together and tightly gripping the barrel ends in which a groove has been cut to hold their ends.

The hoops, of iron or, in the case of special barrels, of "Best Staffordshire Steel", are hand wrought because they have to be accommodated to curved sides that also slope inwards or outwards. They are placed on while still hot, and hammered into position with a heavy cooper's

One of the cooper's skills—the shaping of the iron or steel hoops which, placed on the barrel while hot, shrink as they cool to clamp it completely watertight. The metal hoops must be perfectly shaped to fit the curve of the barrel.

hammer and a "drift"—a wedge-shaped block of iron used to ease them into position, under the hammer blows. As they cool, they shrink, thus further constricting the oak staves in a vice-like grip which causes the edges of the staves to be almost "welded" together and absolutely watertight. When the hoops have been placed in position, the temporary hoops, of ash or some other pliable wood, are removed and the spacing of the permanent hoops carefully checked, for there is an exact rule as to their spacing if each hoop is to take the strain for which it was designed. Usually there is a hoop at the very edge of each end of the barrel; a few centimetres from it there will be another hoop, not quite so wide as the end ones. Then, approximately half-way to the "equator" of the barrel, from each end, there will be another hoop. In the case of out-size barrels there may be additional hoops, for the weight of the contents of the barrel will be enormous.

A well-made barrel will last for years and years. It possesses immense strength, and powers of resistance from pressure from outside, from inside, and from either end. When, perhaps after many, many years, the barrel has "started" at some point, and so ceased to be absolutely watertight, it may well have a further length of life as a support for heavy weights in, say, a builder's yard or some similar place. A barrel maker is a craftsman of immense and speci-alised skill; the product of his hands, "heart of oak", has a life in it that may well outlast his own.

Above, the cooper at work with a draw-knife on the circular wooden bottom of a barrel. In the foreground is the long beechwood beam of the "jointer" used to shape the multiple curves of the barrel staves.
Below, placing the completed sets of staves in position for steaming which causes them to bend inwards and close together.

David Lubin was five years old when he first discovered the meaning of poverty and starvation.

One day he was taken by his stepfather, a pedlar in pots and pans, to the home of some poor farm-hands. David was horrified to see the squalor in which the young peasant children lived. They ran around in dirty ragged clothing. They were thin and ill-cared for, and obviously did not get enough to eat.

At first David could not understand how people could live in such dreadful conditions. But as he travelled with his stepfather around the Polish countryside, he saw that most of the peasants were without adequate nourishment—even though their work was growing potatoes, sugar beet, oats and wheat.

David was born in 1850 in a small Polish village. His mother and stepfather were Jewish, and the family had enough money to see that no one starved or ran around half-clothed. Even so, times were hard, and in 1855 David was excited to learn that they were to emigrate to America.

The voyage to New York was a great adventure for David, his two sisters, and his elder brother, Simon. But when they reached America they found almost as much hardship there as they had left behind. The family moved into a cramped and gloomy flat in the East Side of New York, and David's stepfather found work in a nearby factory.

By the time he was nine, David was tired of living in the slums. He had heard of the wonderful climate of California on the West Coast, where the sun always shone and you could grow grapes and oranges. So he left home one morning, and signed on as cabin-boy aboard the *Sonora,* bound for San Francisco.

He told the captain he was twelve years old, and was just about to sail when his brother Simon rushed onto the ship. Simon and David's two sisters, Jeanette and Fanny, had been scouring the streets in search of the runaway. When the captain heard that David was only aged nine, he immediately ordered him ashore.

When the captain found out that David was only nine he ordered him ashore.

So, for the time being, David's dream of living and farming in California came to an end. But he vowed that one day he *would* reach the "Sunshine State", and when he did he would have his own farm on which none of the workers would ever go short of food or money.

For the next few years David dutifully attended school. When he was fourteen he got his first job, as a factory errand boy. He next worked in a jewellery factory, where he invented a new way of soldering together sunglasses.

All the while his ambition to see California grew stronger. And in 1865, when he was sixteen, he told his mother and stepfather that he was joining a wagon train in Independence, Missouri. The covered wagons were making for the Great Salt Lake in Utah, and from there he would travel south-west to San Francisco and then down to Los Angeles.

Despite his mother's misgivings, he took a train to Independence, and a few days later was sitting next to the driver of a covered wagon, wearing a cowboy hat and neckerchief. As the settlers moved through Kansas and into Indian territory they took extra precautions, and at night formed the wagons into a circle in case of attack.

When he finally reached Los Angeles, David soon learnt how to swim, shoot, and ride a horse. This last pastime almost cost him his life when a pony he was riding became trapped in a desert quicksand. As the pony sank helplessly in the sand David remembered that the only way to escape was to keep moving. He forced the pony to struggle forward, and after an anxious five minutes succeeded in reaching firm ground.

But even the narrow escape did not quench David's spirit of adventure.

Before long he joined a party of gold prospectors bound for the Vulture Mine near Yuma, Arizona. The men did not find any gold, but they did have their share of excitement. One night they were attacked by Apache Indians, and David, who was on guard, was wounded in the leg by an arrow.

After this he worked for a time as a lamp salesman in New Orleans, and then became a stoker aboard the steamboat *Natchez.* He worked on the *Natchez* during its famous race up the Mississippi to St Louis against the *Robert E. Lee.* The *Natchez* was beaten by 3½ hours, despite the efforts of David and his fellow stokers who worked stripped to the waist in the engine-room until they almost dropped.

David's next important venture came in 1875, when he became one of the first men in America to operate a "one-price" store. In those days it was customary for people to wander into the shops and bargain for whatever they wanted. But in his store in Sacramento David refused to knock a cent off, or put a cent on.

No Lies

In a newspaper advertisement he asked shopkeepers to "Turn over a new leaf—be HONEST—learn the true value of goods, and do not misrepresent; and do not lie to the public."

His policy of selling "at ONE PRICE only" soon brought him plenty of customers. He saved his money carefully, got married, raised a family and at last bought his own fruit ranch near Sacramento, the capital of Central California. True to his resolution, he treated his workers with kindness and respect.

"Gruff commands, surly orders, poor food and a dirty bed," he stated, "are not likely to produce faithful and conscientious workers."

Then, in 1886, he started his campaign on behalf of farmers and the people who bought and ate their produce. He believed that the fierce competition that existed between farmers brought about "barbarism and robbery." And he told a gathering of world agriculturists that, "We should aim to cultivate that which will be of advantage to our neighbours, and in this we will most surely find our own highest advantage."

Prompted by his childhood memories of starvation, he later went to

WHO WENT WEST

Europe where he unsuccessfuly tried to interest the French President and King Edward VII of Britain in his scheme for feeding the poor and needy. Finally, on 24th October, 1904, he gained an audience with King Victor Emmanuel III of Italy. The monarch listened to his scheme for world food distribution, and promised to have it examined by his ministers.

The scheme was accepted, and a building to house the new International Institute of Agriculture was erected in the Borghese Gardens in Rome. Later the Institute became part of the League of Nations. It continued its work of food conservation and distribution, and in 1945 it was incorporated in the United Nations Food and Agricultural Organisation, which deals with world hunger and food shortage.

Today the work started by David Lubin, who died in 1918, is being carried out with even greater intensity. It is his memorial, and it ensures that his foresight and humanity will never be forgotten.

As the pony sank slowly into the quicksand, David urged it forward to the firmer ground . . .

STRANGE CREATURES

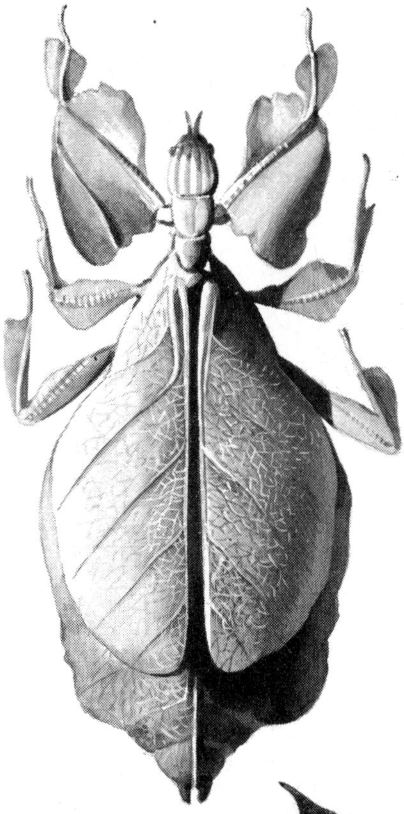

COAT OF MANY COLOURS

There are many different kinds of chameleon, a strange little creature which lives on insects. It catches these with a tongue almost as long as its body. The tongue lashes out very quickly and the insect is caught on the sticky blob at the tip.

The greatest curiosity, though, and the one for which the chameleon is bestknown, is its ability to change colour when necessary to blend in with its surroundings. Its eyes, which are set in turrets, can rotate independently so that the chameleon can see danger coming from any direction.

OUT TO FOOL YOU

Shown above are two particularly amazing insects which have the ability to camouflage themselves very successfully. You may not even recognise where the insect stops and the plant on which it is sitting begins!

The insect at the top is a leaf insect which lives in India. You will see how cleverly hidden it is as it sits in full view on a leaf. Apart from its appearance it has a habit of trembling slightly in the same way that a leaf would.

The thorn insect below it is another intriguing example of the way in which Nature equips tiny, otherwise vulnerable creatures with the means to protect themselves. You will see that the thorn insect looks exactly like a thorn. And when it is sitting on a thorn twig it always faces the same way, so that even on close inspection it is difficult to see that there is, in fact, an insect there at all.

HEADS OR TAILS?

Another curious creature is the great anteater, which measures about 2 metres from end to end, for its tiny head seems quite unimportant beside its bushy tail. It is grey and brown in colour, the hindquarters being darker in tone than elsewhere on the body, and the creature has a bold black pattern, outlined in white, on the throat and shoulders. It lives on the plains and in the forests of South Africa.

It has strong claws on its forelegs, and, to help keep these sharp for digging out the termites on which it feeds, the anteater walks on its knuckles. The anteater has a long thin tongue with which it catches the termites.

FLY WITH THE LONG NECK

Inside dead or decaying wood, perhaps even in the logs in you garden shed, lives the snake fly. It lays its eggs in the decaying wood and its larvae feed on the creatures which are to be found living under bark. The snake fly is not a true fly. In fact, it gets its name from the long neck which gives it some resemblance to a snake. You may think that even this is an unsatisfactory description, for the head and body do not seem to fit together and the creature looks as if it has changed heads with something else. The adult fly has a wingspan of just under 2.5 centimetres, which is quite large for a fly, so you might look out for it.

DON'T GO BY APPEARANCES!

This fly is one of a relatively small order. The Latin name for it is *Mecoptera*, and the common name is scorpion fly. When one looks at this insect it is easy to see how it got its common name, for it looks extremely ferocious in the same way that a scorpion does. But there is, in fact, no need to worry should you meet one in your garden during the summer. Despite its fearsome appearance it is completely harmless.

There are six families in this order, of which two are known to be world-wide, two live in Australia, one occurs in Europe and North America, and the sixth is purely American.

EGGS ON STILTS

You would be more likely to see the fly on the left than either of the two above, for it often enters houses and may be found resting on window ledges or flying lazily around the room even in mid-winter. It is the lacewing fly, or, to give it its Latin name, *Neuroptera*. The unusual thing about it is the way it lays its eggs, for, as you can see in our illustration, these eggs are laid at the end of a stalk which is attached to a tree or shrub. The larvae feed on greenfly, so the lacewing fly usually lays its eggs in a place inhabited by greenfly. Although the larvae feed on greenfly, the adult lacewing fly eats little or nothing at all.

A LONG-DISTANCE TAIL

The Japanese long-tailed cock is not a truly natural bird but is an example of what perversions of nature man can cultivate when the fancy takes him. For many centuries, on the Japanese island of Shikokee, this bird has been bred to increase the length of its tail. At present the record is held by a cock whose tail measures no less than 11 metres! It seems rather unfair on these creatures that man should thus amuse himself.

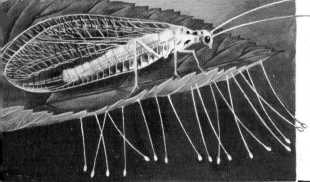

THE WELL-EQUIPPED GARDENER

The mole cricket is a British insect which is seldom seen, for it is found in only a few areas of the country. Another reason why it is not often seen is that it spends nearly all its time in a burrow underground. Like the mole it is well-equipped for such a life. The first pair of legs have developed into efficient digging organs, as you will note in the enlarged section of our illustration.

The four pointed extensions are digging implements, rather like a garden fork! The hard, blade-like teeth above them are used in the same manner as one would use a pair of shears for such purposes as severing roots.

PUTTING ON A PLAY

It starts as an idea in a playwright's head and ends months later when the final curtain falls on the first night of a new play in London's West End. In between there have been rehearsals, conferences and crises. Putting on a play is a major operation.

To simplify things and show a typical way of staging a play, let us invent one called *The Frightened Mice,* which a young playwright, Bill Shakeshawe, has written. Bill sends it to a literary agent who decides that, unlike most plays he receives, this one has possibilities. He sends it to a theatrical management called Pangloss Productions, who snap it up.

Mr Pangloss decides that the play, a thriller about a group of people trapped in a lonely house on Dartmoor, knowing that one of them is a murderer, needs a big star to give it a good chance of success.

"Why not Mary Woodlock?" suggests his No. 2, mentioning the name of a popular film star who is also an excellent actress. A phone call to her agent reveals that she has almost finished a film and will probably say yes if she likes the part. She does.

Pangloss signs a top director, Peter Guthbrook, to stage the play, which means far more than simply telling the actors where to move: he will have to interpret the author's intentions

On a bare stage, lit only by a working light, a rehearsal is in progress. In the foreground the stage manager is speaking to the director, sitting "out front" in the empty auditorium.

Whether the play is a period one or a modern drama, costume fittings are a vital part of the rehearsal period.

The first night is over and cast and audience alike salute the leading lady.

and is the key figure in putting on a play.

He is brought into a "casting" conference. These are six rôles to be filled besides Mary's, five male and one female.

Meanwhile, backers have been found to put up the several thousand pounds needed for the production.

A designer is hired, though, as the play has only one scene—a baronial hall used as a sitting-room cum dining-room—he will not have all that much to do. Pangloss also hire a stage manager, who will be in charge backstage and act as company manager and whose duties will include paying the cast.

He chooses a deputy stage manager (D.S.M.) and an assistant (A.S.M.), not long out of her drama school, very keen, and destined to be the company dogsbody at a small weekly salary. Her duties include making coffee and tea at rehearsals.

Rehearsals take place in the actual theatre where it will be performed, which is lucky for the cast, who would otherwise use rehearsal rooms or other theatres. The scenery for the current Pangloss play is "struck", to be reassembled each evening, and a few basic bits of furniture serve the cast until the final rehearsals when the actual setting will be used.

The very first rehearsal is a reading of the play, followed by a discussion of the characters. During one break the cast are shown a model of the setting that the designer has made; in another the company's Press Representative appears, meets the cast, and has a chat with Mary Woodlock about publicity. It is up to him to get as much as possible about the play into the papers *before* it opens.

Over the next few days Peter Guthbrook "blocks" the play, which means he tells the cast where and when they must move about the stage. He knows just what he wants—unlike some directors!—but he is open to suggestions from his cast, who all read from their scripts for at least a week, some for longer. Gradually, the play begins to take shape and the characters become "real".

The D.S.M. and A.S.M. take it in turn to be on "the Book", or Prompt Script, in which all moves are noted and from which prompts are given when the actors forget their lines, or "dry". When not on the Book they rush around collecting "props"— stage properties—such as cigarette cases, suitcases, clocks, a revolver, etc., that are needed in the play.

Two understudies, a man and a woman, are hired. The man "covers" two of the cast in case of illness, the woman, Mary Woodlock, whose part is enormous. The other men are covered by the D.S.M., the woman by the A.S.M. It is almost impossible fitting in understudy rehearsals at this stage, but it has to be done.

A wardrobe mistress arrives to look after clothes and iron shirts. Everyone provides his own clothes except the policeman, whose uniform is hired, and Mary Woodlock, who is sent to the most famous fasion designer in London at the Management's expense.

Suddenly, crisis strikes in the last week of rehearsals. Guthbrook decides that a scene in the last act needs rewriting; and Bill Shakeshawe, who has tactfully kept away from rehearsals until this final week, sits up all one night frantically rewriting.

Next day the actors have an awful time, altering their scripts and their moves, and learning their new lines. But the changes work and Bill Shakeshawe heaves a sigh of relief.

On the Saturday night the current play ends and the next morning the theatre's stagehands put up *The Frightened Mice* set and a rehearsal of the play's lighting changes takes place, followed that evening by the dress rehearsal. This drags on until 3 a.m. and includes some sharp words between director and stage management when a revolver shot fails to go off. After being given "notes" on their performances the cast stagger home, to return in the afternoon for a run-through of the play in ordinary clothes.

The two previews go well, but first night nerves afflict the actors on opening night. Their dressing-room walls are filled with telegrams and good luck cards.

Guthbrook and the author, their work over, wish the cast luck and are wished luck in return. "Act I Beginners, please!" calls the A.S.M. into a microphone in the "prompt corner" at the side of the stage. The plays begins . . .

THE PEOPLE BEHIND A PLAY . . .

Author   Agent   Director   Producer

Leading lady   Leading man   Supporting cast and understudies   Designer   Stage manager

Deputy stage manager   Assistant stage manager

AND THERE ARE OTHER KEY FIGURES

Wardrobe mistress and dressers

Carpenter, props man, stagehands, etc, orchestra, if required, front of house staff, manager, usherettes . . .

THE POWER OF THE BORGIAS

In the early hours of the morning, one July day in 1497, Giorgio the waterman sat alongside his boat on the banks of the River Tiber. The moon was up, yet the streets of Rome were parched from the heat of an unusually hot summer's day. Giorgio could not sleep and lay on the ground, full-length, gazing idly across the dark waters.

Out of the shadows two men appeared, walking cautiously along the path beside the river. They stopped some distance from Giorgio, peering right and left before beckoning quickly into the darkness behind them. Giorgio judged it wise to remain quiet and unobserved. He knew it did not pay to be curious: too many cut-throats and assassins roamed the streets at night. Even as the thought crossed his mind, four more men appeared, one richly clad and riding a white horse.

The party stopped at the river's edge and Giorgio was close enough to see the limp corpse of a man draped across the horse's back. Close enough, too, to hear the man on the horse addressed by another as "Your Eminence." The body was tumbled to the ground, its legs and arms grabbed by two men, who swung it back and forth a couple of times and then tossed it far out into the river. After a moment, a dark object appeared floating on the surface. Again a voice spoke, muted but loud enough to be overheard. "'Tis the Duke's cloak, Your Eminence." Then the men took stones and threw them at the cloak until it sank out of sight. In a moment all the figures had disappeared back into the shadows and the waters were still. "Your Eminence"—twice had Giorgio heard the words—and this was the title of a cardinal of Rome!

When Giorgio finally plucked up courage to report what he had seen to the police, there was already a hue and cry in Rome over the disappearance of Giovanni, Duke of Gandia. Giorgio's story spread quickly to the Vatican and to the ears of Giovanni's father, Pope Alexander VI. He ordered the Tiber to be dragged. Two hundred fishermen scoured the river's depths with nets and poles for several hours, until a body was found jammed against the sewage pipes, pierced with numerous dagger-thrusts and its throat slit.

It was the missing Duke, whose family name was Borgia—a notorious

Lucrezia Borgia.

name, borne too by his brother, the dreaded Cesare. Cesare had been created an archbishop at the age of 16 by his father, and a cardinal a year later, and was thus entitled to be called "Your Eminence."

Popular history has made the House of Borgia a symbol for all things evil. Their women have been described as heartless poisoners and their men as monsters of wickedness. And no member of the family has so bad a name as Cesare Borgia. The murder of his brother Giovanni is only one of a long list of crimes attributed to him.

SEARCH FOR POWER

As a family, the Borgias enjoyed, enormous power in 15th-century Rome. They were Spanish noblemen who came to Italy in 1443, and the first of them to gain prominence was Alphonso de Borgia, who became Pope Calixtus III. He created his nephew Rodrigo a cardinal, and he, in his turn, became pope as Alexander VI. Alexander was a man of outstanding ability—corrupt, pleasure-loving, and consumed with ambition for wealth and even greater power than his supreme office afforded him. He was passionately devoted to his many children, particularly his son Cesare, and his daughter Lucrezia.

Cesare, who became the image for Machiavelli's typical prince of the Renaissance in his famous book *Il Principe,* was at once handsome, skilful, brave, violent, ambitious and even more corrupt and devious than his father. In command of the churches' armies, he conquered and pillaged throughout Italy, murdering any individual who stood in his way. The verdict of history on this ruthless prince seems to be justified, although the dark deeds of intrigue and murder with which he is associated are shrouded in mystery.

Lucrezia, on the other hand, scarcely deserves her evil reputation, and the melodramatic picture of her as a subtle poisoner is almost certainly nonsense. She was completely dominated by her father and Cesare, and while they lived seemed content to be a willing pawn in their political manoeuvres. She was betrothed to a Spanish nobleman at the age of 11, and by the time she was 22 had survived three marriages and was embarking on her fourth! Her husbands were chosen and disposed of (one of them was murdered by Cesare) according to the demands of the particular alliances Alexander wished to make with influential families. It is significant that when her father died, and she was no longer subject to his endless plans for her future, Lucrezia settled down happily with her fourth husband to a peaceful, uneventful life without a further breath of scandal.

Alexander is reputed to have died, and Cesare to have been brought to the verge of death, by mistakenly drinking poison which had been prepared for a victim. The legend of the Borgia poison, with its stories of poisoned wine and venomous rings which, at the pressure of a hand,

Cesare Borgia: He was created an archbishop at the age of 16.

discharged death, has little foundation in fact.

After his father's death, Cesare's world crumbled. One of his enemies became pope and he was compelled to give up most of his possessions. He was killed fighting in an insignificant war, still only 32 years of age. But, above all else, the Renaissance period was an age of youth. Life moved quickly, and at 16 one had already tasted many of its pleasures and glories. It was a time when great artists produced their masterpieces at the age of 20 and cardinals were created at 17.

Amid the turbulent and terrible record of the lives of the Borgias, it is as well to remember that one member of the family achieved spiritual eminence, and that was Francis Borgia (1510-72), a Roman Catholic saint and general of the order of the Jesuits, who lived a life of simple monasticism.

Crouching low to avoid being seen, Giorgio the boatman saw the body swung backwards and forwards and then hurled into the dark waters of the River Tiber . . .

65

FAIR PLAY FOR FIGHTERS

In the freezing winter cold of an open common, two men fought viciously, butting and gouging at each other, while the crowd of dandies, bullies and bruisers cheered them on. But one man who did not cheer was Jack Broughton, the boxing champion of England. He was disgusted; and as he watched, he was thinking out a set of rules which would make boxing a fairer sport.

The year was 1741. Only a few months earlier, Broughton himself had fought in similar conditions against a Yorkshireman named George Stevenson, who died as the result of his injuries. Broughton had vowed he would never fight again until the rules were changed. Now he was drawing up the new rules himself.

Today, very few people have heard of Broughton. The man who is remembered for writing the Rules of Boxing more or less as we know them today is John Sholto Douglas, the 8th Marquess of Queensberry.

But we remember the wrong man!

To discover why, it is necessary to take a look at the century of boxing which followed the publication of Broughton's Rules in 1743.

The new rules were not popular at first among the professsional bruisers or the rough crowds which came to watch them fight. Rule 7, for example, read, "That no person is to hit his adversary when he is down, or seize him by the ham or breeches, or any part below the waist. A man on his knees is to be reckoned down." This outlawed the old trick of tripping an opponent and then mauling him severely before he could get to his feet.

Under the London Prize Ring Rules introduced in 1838, restrictions were tightened further, but it was still possible for a man to leave the ring maimed for life. It was the boxers' own "trade union" which drew up these rules, revised them 15 years later, and again in 1866.

By then, boxing had ceased to be a purely professional sport. A 23-year-old amateur boxer, John Graham Chambers, set up the Amateur Athletic Club in London, at which boxers fought for the fun of winning, with no money at stake, and no wish to injure their opponents for the sake of the crowd.

NEW SET OF RULES

To Chambers, the old rules were abominable. He wrote new ones, introducing the three-minute round and the use of properly padded gloves, and outlawing the use of spring heels in boots or shoes.

He had some support, for the savagery of the prize fights had led to frequent intervention by the police. But to have his rules accepted, Chambers needed help. It was one thing for a promising young fighter to write new rules. It was an entirely different matter for him to win publicity for them.

What Chambers needed was a man of influence behind him.

The man he approached was the Marquess of Queensberry. Virtually all that Queensberry did was to sign his name on the list of rules!

These rules were revised in 1867. In just over a century since then, there have been minor changes and adaptations, but their basic principle remains unaltered—that the object of boxing is to win, not to injure. These are the rules which, with a few local variations, are now in use throughout the world.

And—wrongly—these basic laws of fair play in the ring are known as the Queensberry Rules. The man whose name they ought to bear is, of course, John Graham Chambers.

This Greek vase shows boxers in action. The sport was known to both the early Greeks and Romans.

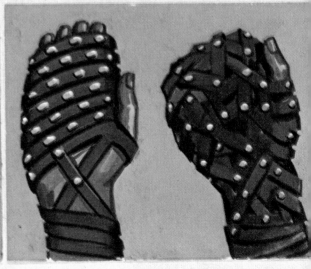
Early forms of boxing gloves. Called cesti, they were made of strips of leather often studded with metal.

Below: an advertisement for an early bare-fist prize fight. The poster is by William Hogarth, who painted the portraits of many famous fighters of the bare-fist era.

Jack Broughton was known as "the father of British boxing". He took part in many contests himself (top) and introduced the use of boxing gloves, although he often fought bare-fisted himself.

Police breaking up an outdoor boxing match.

It was boxer James Figg, above, who encouraged Jack Broughton to take up boxing.

TERROR OF

In the summer of 1900, the whole Western world waited anxiously for news from Peking. All foreigners in the famous Chinese city—over 3,000 of them—were under siege in the Western legations there. And for 55 days they held out gallantly until a relief force of British, Russian, American and French forces arrived.

All stories grow with the telling, and this one became an epic of heroic fortitude by the time news of Peking's relief reached the outside world. The "yellow devils" had been crushed; everyone in the siege seemed to have a vainglorious tale to tell; and a determination to keep the primitive, treacherous Oriental down grew fiercer.

A study of contemporary accounts shows a somewhat different story. Certainly there was a rebellion, people were killed and there was a good deal of damage—for which China had to pay £1,000,000—but the whole thing was exaggerated.

Today, the rebellion might even have found many supporters in the West, for China had suffered as the Western powers scrambled to claim her territories. An uprising was almost predictable. It came, and was called the Boxer Rebellion.

"The Boxers" was the nickname given to the fanatical anti-foreign secret society that had triggered off the rebellion. More correctly known as the "Fists for Righteous Harmony," they were a mystical organisation said to be descended from other ancient Chinese secret associations and who believed themselves invulnerable and endowed with various supernatural powers.

That their uprising was suppressed shows they were anything but invulnerable—but they were actually effective in Western eyes for one very definite reason. They were a secret society, a foreign secret society, and an Oriental secret society!

Since that "Boxer" uprising, the whole world has had a ready-made band of bogey-men ready to hand. Almost everyone has a mental picture of the "Terror of the Tongs," in which sinister Chinamen strike from the shadows of night with ritual hatchets and then pad silently away to visit their next victim.

Probably we have the cinema to thank for this picture. During the early days of film-making, there were any number showing celluloid heroes bedevilled by Oriental secret societies. They made such an impact that, during the early 1900s, some sensitive Chinamen on America's West Coast even closed down their laundries and restaurants because film-going sightseers came in their hundreds to gape at these "dread denizens" of crime and terror.

Even so, Hollywood only helped to make more people aware of Tong terror. And, though it may have embellished the Chinese secret societies, it certainly did not invent them. They were—and are—all too real.

What is more, they have been far more successful than many other secret societies in remaining . . . secret. Very few outsiders have penetrated their mysteries.

SECRET SOCIETIES

The reason for this lies in Chinese history. The rule of that country has always been rather cruel and oppressive; and it is in such circumstances that secret societies thrive. So it was, broadly speaking, that membership of a secret society became ingrained in the Chinese way of life.

The earliest records of these societies date back almost two thousand years to when the *Carnation Eyebrows*, who painted their faces in weird and alarming patterns, attempted to overthrow the emperor of the time. They were only overthrown when loyalist troops painted their faces in the same way and defeated the society in the resulting confusion.

From that time on, the growth and spread of Chinese secret societies becomes complicated.

They might be formed to fight *for* something or *against* something; but there would often be a situation where two societies might be fighting *for* a common aim and at the same time *against* each other because of another aim.

However, these societies did depend for their existence on secrecy, and sacred rituals helped to ensure that superstitious devotees kept the secrets. That the rituals were impressive and the punishments for breaking vows hideous is obvious, for no one yet knows what they were.

Names like the Copper Horses, Yellow Turbans, Illustrious Worthies, the White Cloud Society, the Three Incense Sticks, the Eight Diagrams, and, of course, the Fists for Righteous Harmony, stud Chinese history, and there are alarming tales attached to all of them.

But by far the most noteworthy and notorious was the White Lotus Society. This may date from the 4th century, though it was in the 14th century that it came to prominence. At that time Kublai Kahn ruled China, and Chinese resistance to his rule was kept alive by a rumour that a certain omen would signify the country's freedom.

When stirs the one-eyed man of stone, This dynasty shall be overthrown.

Possibly the White Lotus Society coined the rhyme and started the rumour, but when in 1344 workmen repairing the banks of the Yellow River dug up the stone statue of a one-eyed man, the news swept the country. Rebellion followed, and by 1368 Kublai Khan and his Mongols were unseated. There started a new dynasty—named the Ming by the Society.

This Ming Dynasty lasted until the mid-17th century, and throughout the period the White Lotus Society was rarely heard of. But then came the rule of the Manchus, and once again the White Lotus appeared.

Since then the name has kept appearing and disappearing—though when it has disappeared it has probably only changed its name. It is said that its object is to restore the Ming; but as Ming also means "Light" as well as the name of the dynasty, this objective has been taken by many to mean that the society wants to gain power for itself.

Since the 20th century secret societies have not been as important as political powers, though it is known that Mao Tse-Tung, the great leader of Red China who died in 1976, used them when his Communists seized power in the country.

Activities of the societies have not been confined to China. In America, where they were called the Tongs, after a Chinese word meaning "meeting place," they were active as far back as the 1850s.

THE TONGS

In China and abroad, the Tongs built up a huge empire of crime, and hired killers to liquidate those who dared to oppose them.

LAND OF LEGEND

The storytellers of Ancient Greece kept their listeners enthralled with their tales of gods and goddesses, mighty men and monsters, wanderers and lovely women. Some, like Helen of Troy and Odysseus, may have been real people, others are completely mythical, but all of them are part of mankind's heritage

Zeus was chief of all the Greek gods; the Romans knew him as Jove or Jupiter. The course of all human affairs was directed by him, and his throne and the seat of the rest of the gods was on Mount Olympus. He was lord of the winds and rain and of thunder and lightning, and he is usually portrayed holding thunderbolts and with a crown of leaves. There are innumerable stories about him and his wife Hera, who was jealous of his interest in other goddesses and mortal women. Zeus knew everything and saw everything, and the Greeks regarded him as a kindly ruler who was often capable of pity as well as wrath. He was the god of the family, of friendship and the god-protector of all Greece.

THE MAGIC WATERS

Before his adventure with the Sirens, Odysseus had been a leading Greek commander at the siege of Troy and had been partly responsible for the death of Rhesus, King of Thrace, who owned some fine white horses. An oracle had said that if these horses drank the waters of the River Xanthus, Troy would never be taken. So when Rhesus and his men were marching to help Troy, he was killed and his horses driven off.

ODYSSEUS AND THE SONG OF THE SIRENS

One of the hero Odysseus's adventures sailing home from Troy was his encounter with the Sirens—sea-nymphs who lured sailors to their doom. Warned about them by an enchantress, Odysseus had himself lashed to the mast of his ship when they started singing their Siren song. His men's ears were stopped with wax. So they escaped the fate of other sailors whose bones lay at the Sirens' feet.

THE FOOLISH CRIME OF KING TANTALUS

Everyone has been tantalised in their time, including the man who was first to suffer—Tantalus! He was a king who had been invited to dinner with the gods on Mount Olympus, where he rashly stole their nectar and ambrosia. For this and other tactless crimes—including serving up his own son as a dish for the gods to test their divinity—he was put waist-deep in a lake with delicious fruit above him that he could never reach. And when he wanted to drink, the water always receded. Meanwhile, his son was returned to life by the gods and was exactly as before, except for a portion of shoulder that an absent-minded god had nibbled. It was replaced by ivory! Meanwhile his father went on being tantalised.

THE FLAME OF FEAR

Meleager was seven days old when the Fates decreed he would die when a lighted brand on the family fire burnt out. His mother Althaea quenched the flame before the brand had had time to burn out, and hid it. Later, when he was a grown man, Meleager killed his uncles after they had stolen a boar's hide he had given the lovely Atalanta. His enraged mother threw the fatal brand on a fire. Meleager died at once; Althaea killed herself.

THE PUNISHMENT OF HERCULES

As a punishment for murder, the invincible hero Hercules was forced by the Oracle of Delphi to perform 12 labours. The 11th was to fetch the golden apples of the Hesperides, which grew on Mt. Atlas, where Atlas himself held up the world. Accounts vary, but one has the hero persuading Atlas to fetch the apples while Hercules held up the world! When Atlas brought the three apples back he did not feel like resuming his burden! Hercules managed to trick him into taking the world back and escaped with the apples. Another version has him killing a dragon to get the apples. On the way home he killed a giant. For the record, the Greeks called him Heracles, but Hercules is his better known Roman name.

JASON AND THE SEARCH FOR THE FABULOUS FLEECE

Jason was the leader of an expedition which set out in a ship called the *Argo* to find the Golden Fleece. Among the Argonauts who accompanied him were Orpheus and Hercules. After many adventures they came to the Kingdom of Aeëtes, who admitted he had the Fleece but refused to give it up unless Jason peformed two dangerous tasks. Luckily for Jason, the King's daughter Medea fell in love with him and, being a marvellous magician, helped him. So Jason and Medea reached the Fleece and he slew the ferocious dragon that guarded it and seized the trophy. Jason and Medea lived happily for ten years, but he fell in love with someone else, which is another legend!

THE WILD WINDS

Legend has it that the winds lived in the Aeolian Isles, guarded by Aeolus. When Odysseus called at the home of Aeolus on his long voyage home, Aeolus gave him a wine-skin full of all contrary winds which might impede his voyage. Alas, Odysseus's companions were so curious that they opened the skin and the winds flew out. A return visit to Aeolus was not so successful: he refused to help again.

THE BEAUTY WHO WAS TURNED INTO A BEAST

Medusa was a beautiful maiden, famous for her hair, who, as a punishment, had her hair turned to serpents and her face made so ugly that anyone who looked at her became stone. She was also given wings and brazen claws. She was the leader of the Gorgons, women who had suffered the same fate. A young hero named Perseus was sent to fetch Medusa's head. Fortunately for him, the goddess Athena gave him a polished shield so he would see only Medusa's reflection, and Hermes gave him a sickle and other aids, including winged sandals. He flew to the Gorgons' lair and beheaded Medusa. From her body sprang the winged horse Pegasus and the warrior Chrysaor. Perseus escaped in an invisible helmet.

THE RAM WHO CAME TO THE RESCUE

Phrixus and Helle were the children of Athamas and Nephele, but Athamas, who had been ordered to marry Nephele by a goddess, really loved another! Complications led to his nearly sacrificing his children, who were saved just in time when a god sent a flying ram with a golden fleece to carry them off. Poor Helle fell in the straits between Europe and Asia now called the Hellespont, but Phrixus escaped.

74

TERRIFYING TURTLE

A great ball of iron hurtled into the courtyard of the castle. While a group of soldiers were looking at it, the ball exploded and killed 30 of them.

The killer was a bomb, a new weapon in the 16th century, when this incident happened. The soldiers it killed were Japanese and the men who threw it were Koreans.

Yi Jang-son, who invented it, gave it to his compatriots to drive out the Japanese who, for six years from 1592, sent hordes of soldiers—350,000 of them—to conquer Korea.

Gunpowder had been known and used for a long time. But the exploding shell was something the Japanese had not seen before. However, it was not nearly so startling as a fresh horror which beset a large Japanese fleet trying to go to the relief of its countrymen in Korea.

The sailors saw a monster, shaped like a giant turtle and as large as a ship, coming swiftly towards them over the water.

Blasts of flame spurted from its dragon's head, above which horns protruded. The flames were fired by a rocket gun made of bronze.

Along its sides were ports. From these projected long oars which rowed the strange craft over the surface of the sea. Through other ports above these, cannon were fired at the Japanese.

Once again, the inventive Koreans had made a new weapon of war, probably the world's first ironclad warship.

This monster, and others like it, helped the Koreans to drive the Japanese from their country.

THE BEAST OF THUNDER

Anyone who has seen a rhinoceros lumbering through the swampy jungles of Africa and Asia might well imagine himself back in the prehistoric world of millions of years ago, when huge and monstrous-looking animals roamed the land.

It may seem strange that the nearest relation of the ugly and ungainly rhinoceros is the graceful horse. But if we study the history of animals in the fossil remains of their ancestors who lived thousands of centuries ago, we find that at one period the rhinoceros had a very horse-like ancestor indeed.

This was the huge Baluchitherium, which was 8.5 metres long and stood 5.4 metres high. It had a head and tail very like those of a horse, but instead of hoofs its broad and heavy feet had toes encased in hoof-like nails.

The Baluchitherium was not the most distant ancestor of the rhinoceros. It lived about twenty-five million years ago in a period of time called the Middle Oligocene.

It is not until we go back fifty million years to the prehistoric period called the Eocene, that we find animals really like the rhinoceros of today.

One of the biggest and most terrifying-looking was the Uintatherium. According to its fossil remains, the Uintatherium was about twice the size of a modern rhinoceros and its body was much the same shape as that of an elephant. It also had short tusks, but on its head were six horns arranged in pairs.

In spite of its great size, the Uintatherium was a vegetarian, which fed on the soft and juicy plants growing beside the swamps and rivers in which it spent much of its time. It was native to what we now call North America.

Another rhinoceros-like creature that lived at the same time and also belonged to North America was the Brontotherium. It was somewhat smaller than the Uintatherium, and had a two-pronged horn growing from the top of its nose.

Bones of the Brontotherium were often washed out of the ground by rain and found by the Sioux Indians. The Indians called them the remains of the "thunder horses", which once upon a time hunted bison in thunderstorms and killed them with their huge hoofs. So scientists called the rhinoceros-like creature "Brontotherium", which means "beast of thunder."

About the time that the Brontotherium was roaming the plains of Nebraska and Dakota, another ancestor of the rhinoceros was making its home along the banks of the Nile in Egypt.

This was the Arsinoitherium, a huge creature 4.2 metres long and 2.5 metres high. Like the Brontotherium, it had a two-pronged horn.

Each of the prongs was flat and had a sharp edge like a sword. It was also a vegetarian and only used its horns in self defense.

Although the rhinoceros of today is a pygmy compared with its gigantic ancestors, it is, with the exception of the elephant, still the largest animal on Earth.

There are five species of rhinoceros, of which the largest is the so-called white rhinoceros of Africa, whose real colour is a dirty grey rather than white. The Indian rhinoceros has a greyish-black skin arranged in great folds like plates of armour.

The ancient Mexicans worshipped the sun, regarded the moon as his wife, and the stars as his sisters. The "feathered snake" shown on the side of this temple is the emblem of Quetzalcoatl, the god of the air, and thus of breath and of life. This temple, at Teotihuacan, near modern Mexico City, was periodically visited by the great Montezuma as an act of pilgrimage.

WHERE THE AZTECS SPOKE TO THEIR GODS

The Aztec people were proud and warlike but their strange religious beliefs led to their defeat by the Spaniards

When the Spanish conquerors burst upon Mexico in the first half of the sixteenth century, they found the Aztecs—an American Indian tribe with a highly developed civilisation—in occupation.

The centre of Aztec power at that time was the twin lake cities of Tenochtitlan and Tlaltelolco. One of the Spanish conquerors wrote down his first impressions of it:

"When we arrived at the great market place we were astounded at the number of people and the quality of goods that it contained, and at the good order and control that was maintained, for we had never seen such things before . . .

"Every kind of merchandise was

kept by itself and had its fixed place marked out. There were dealers in gold, silver, and precious stones, feathers, mantles and embroidered goods. Then there were Indian slaves; they brought some along tied to poles, with collars about their necks so that they could not escape, while others they let free.

BUSY TRADERS

"There were traders selling pieces of cloth and cotton and articles of twisted thread, and sellers of cocoa, ropes, sandals, sweet cooked roots and all kinds of foodstuffs."

There was gold used as money, too, and gold was what the Spanish conquerors were looking for.

Their eyes gleamed when they saw "this gold placed in thin quills of the geese of the country, white quills, so that the gold shows through, and according to the length and thickness of the quills they arrange their accounts with one another, setting the value of so many mantles or so many gourds of cocoa."

The Aztecs had probably arrived in this region of Mexico about four hundred years before the Spanish invaders. They were then a warlike tribe of wandering hunters and they decided to settle down and fortify the Tenochtitlan island.

CITY SITE

This island was in a vast lake which, hard though it is to believe, is today the site of Mexico City, one of the world's largest cities. The water has gone, and where the lake and the island once stood is now home to thirty million people. But 450 years ago, the Spanish conquerors had to cross a narrow causeway across the lake to get to Tenochtitlan island and marvel at the wonderful sights in the market place of the Aztec capital.

On the causeway and on the canals which served as streets plied a multitude of canoes filled with short, brown-skinned people. The houses in the island city were painted a shining white or rich red, and they were dominated by a multitude of towering, temple-crowned pyramids. Round about the city were strange "floating gardens"—in reality artificial islands of mud scraped from the floor of the lake, where food-plants and herbs were grown.

The Aztecs lived mainly by farming and maize was their chief food, as it is of their modern descendants. But among them were expert craftsmen, including masons and sculptors, jewellers, potters and weavers.

For a long time they had been a warlike nation, and had been greatly enriched with tribute from subject races. Records of the tribute, as well as histories and sacred almanacs, were

Part of the decorated front of the Temple of Quetzalcoatl at Teotihuacan. Here the serpent-heads of the god are prominent. The seashells, are symbolic of Quetzalcoatl. Their spiral form typifies the eddies of the wind, with which the god was associated.

This jaguar mural on a Teotihuacan temple may be associated with the fact that some of the bravest warriors of the Aztec Empire belonged to an order of knights called the Jaguars. The colours are original and the free-form motion of the animal is quite modern in feeling.

kept in a kind of picture-writing, of which only a few fragments have survived their wholesale destruction by the Spaniards.

BRAVE WARRIORS

The bravest and most successful of their warriors formed three orders of knights, called Eagles, Jaguars and Arrows. The nation was organised in clans, each composed of about 20 families, and a representative of each clan was a member of the supreme council.

The council elected four military chiefs, from among whom two supreme chiefs were chosen. One of these controlled war and foreign affairs, but both had important religious duties, too—in fact, both were chief and priest. Their power was limited, since they could be deposed by the council at any time if they failed in their duties.

When the Spaniards arrived at Tenochtitlan, Montezuma, sometimes described as King or Emperor of the Aztecs, was the reigning war chief. Although the position was not hereditary, it had become customary to elect these chiefs from one family, and the pomp and splendour with which Montezuma was surrounded led the Spaniards to believe that he was an absolute monarch.

The Pyramid of the Sun at Teotihuacan is the most imposing structure left in ancient Mexico. A vast mound, with its great stairways and terraces, it is about 300 metres square at the base, about 30 metres square at the summit and has slopes at an angle of about 45 degrees. It is about 60 metres high and at the summit in Aztec times there was a temple. It is built of adobe, the same material with which the peasant of today builds his mud shack, but the great weight of the structure has compressed the adobe blocks into a solid mass, which is faced with stone and stucco.

It was reported that he was approached with great humility by the highest in the land, and lived in a palace with his two wives in richest splendour attended by thousands of guards and slaves. Acrobats and dwarfs entertained him, and his palace contained beautiful gardens, a menagerie of rare animals, and an extensive swimming pool.

The Spanish, led by Hernando Cortes, were 450-strong whereas the Aztec Empire contained at least ten million people. But in the space of a few short years, that handful of Europeans was to destroy the Aztec Empire and ruin the country.

How, one still wonders, could that possibly have happened? One of the greatest disadvantages the Aztecs faced was certainly their touching faith in their god Quetzalcoatl. This god, believed to be fair-haired and fair-bearded, having taught the Aztecs the art of peace, had sailed away, promising to return some day—in a *ce acatl* month.

By one of the saddest ironies of history, Hernando Cortes happened to be fair-haired and fair-bearded. And he and his companions had marched up the causeway to Tenoch-titlan island in a *ce acatl* month.

Welcoming the enemy they believed to be their god, the Aztecs were acting like the Trojans when they dragged the wooden horse full of enemy Greek soldiers into the heart of their city of Troy. The Spaniards eventually made the Aztec chief Montezuma a hostage, while they looted his empire of its gold and jewellery.

TOTAL COLLAPSE

They formed friendships with other tribes who nursed grievances against Aztec domination and exploited all the internal weaknesses of the great Indian state, until they brought about its total collapse.

When they finally killed Montezuma and the angry Aztecs at last realised that they had been betrayed, the Indians closed in on their tormentors. Even at this stage the Spaniards might have been wiped out, had it not been for a curious belief of the Aztecs.

This was that their gods could be appeased only by the blood of living men, which meant that instead of slaughtering their enemies they had to capture them alive, so that they could sacrifice them to their gods.

Spanish guns and swords were of course very effective weapons against being taken prisoner, and hundreds of Aztecs died because they wanted to capture rather than kill the enemy.

Sometimes in these last desperate days of the siege of Tenochtitlan, the Aztecs did succeed in capturing a few Spaniards alive. Then their gods received their due. The Spanish besiegers, watching helplessly and furiously from afar, saw their companions dragged up the great steps of a pyramid and flung upon the sacrificial stone. There they saw the still-palpitating heart torn from the body opened by the priest's knife.

Small wonder therefore, that after the prolonged and bloody siege of Mexico was over, the common soldiers needed no urging from their own priests to destroy the Aztec temples. Not until the great temples of Tenochtitlan and Tlaltelolco were in ruins, with the images of the gods hurled from the summit, the pyramids little more than rubbish heaps and a Christian church set upon the site of the old altars, was the anger of the Spaniards appeased.

INVADERS FROM ACROSS THE SEA

Top: the Saxon invaders land on the coast of Britain. Above: the outside, and inside, of a typical Saxon hall.

Power was in King Vortigern's mind when he brought two barbarian chiefs to Britain to become his military allies. But the two brothers he chose to help him, Hengest and Horsa, were not content with their role as protectors.

The complete and merciless conquest of Britain began in about the year A.D. 449, when three Saxon longships ground ashore on the coast of Britain at Ebbsfleet in Kent. The countryside at this spot in Pegwell Bay was dreary and melancholy. Between the bold cliffs of Ramsgate and the promontory of South Foreland was a vast, flat space of coarse pasture-land patterned by broad ditches. From the ships, the Jutish chiefs Hengest and Horsa were carried ashore. The Saxon standard of the White Horse was firmly planted in the ground and the first barbarian army to set foot on British soil gathered around it. Strangely enough, these tall, blond warriors had come by invitation, to be greeted as friends by the British ruler, Vortigern.

In the 5th century A.D. the Roman Empire, which included Britain as well as the lands bordering the Mediterranean, was attacked and overrun by hordes of fierce invaders from northern Europe. These barbarian tribes were variously called Saxons, Goths, Huns and Vandals. The Roman legions, which over 350 years before had conquered and occupied Britain, returned to Rome.

The island had enjoyed a long period of peace and prosperity under Roman rule and for a short time this continued. The harvests were good, law and order prevailed, and there seemed no reason to regret the Roman withdrawal. But without the protection of the Roman army, Britain was thrown open not only to internal strife and renewed raids from the Picts and the Irish, but to invasion from the barbarians themselves.

WHEN THE ROMANS LEFT . . .

It was not the Roman custom to teach the people they conquered how to govern and protect themselves, and when the Romans departed the Britons were left helpless. Gildas, an historian who lived in the 6th century and whose writing is the only contemporary British account of the period, records the plea for aid which the British made to the general Actius in Rome:"The barbarians drive us to the sea; the sea throws us back on the barbarians; thus two modes of death await us: we are either slain or drowned."

Vortigern, the Kentish king, saw this danger all too clearly. He knew that his people, ravaged by a mysterious plague that had swept the country, could not resist invasion from any quarter. To protect his power he sought to make an ally of one of his potential enemies and—for a time—succeeded.

Hengest and Horsa and their followers were given an area of land known as the Isle of Thanet in which to make their home. This was later extended to the whole of Kent, which became almost exclusively an area of conquest and settlement for the Jutish people, who themselves became known as Kentishmen. So, peaceably at first, the tribes from the shores of the Baltic—the Saxons, Jutes and Angles—settled in the new land they were later to subdue. Britain was destined to be known as the land of the Angles—Engle-land, or England.

Few periods in the history of Britain have seen as great a change as that which took place during the 150 years following the end of Roman occupation. The whole character of the country was altered dramatically. What was Roman became Teutonic, which is the name given to the Germanic people of the north European coast who "took over" Britain. And no period is more aptly named The Dark Ages, for factual records of historical events are few and the story of England and the coming of the English is one of mystery and legend.

Vortigern's plan to hire Jutish and Saxon warriors as mercenaries, and pit them against the barbaric tribes of Picts and Scots, rebounded on his own head. There can have been little trust between Vortigern and his dangerous allies, and in the course of time the

King Vortigern's death signalled the start of a reign of terror and conquest in Britain.

Jutes and Saxons turned against him. The news of the initial settlement would have spread rapidly, particularly to the bands of Saxon pirates who roamed the seas in search of plunder. More and more longships found their way to Kentish shores and before long the Saxon fighting men abandoned their protective role and attacked the British.

The mercenaries' first aim was to break out of the little corner of Kent in which they were cooped up. This was not easy, as right across their path lay the inlet of sea which at that time cut off Thanet from the mainland. It could only be forded at low tide and at either end it was guarded by the Roman fortresses of Richborough and Reculver. But the crossing was made and the road to London seized.

In 455 a great battle took place at Aylesford during which Horsa was killed and, for the moment, the Jutes and Saxons were halted. How the invaders regained the upper hand is a tale of treachery and cunning which may or may not be true. The story goes that Hengest proposed a peace conference between Vortigern and himself, each to be accompanied by a chosen band of followers. One of the conditions was that all should attend unarmed. Vortigern agreed. When the men were assembled, Hengest gave a signal and his men drew daggers, concealed in their clothing, and stabbed to death Vortigern and every member of his party. The manner of its happening may be legendary, but Vortigern's death signalled the beginning of the complete and bloody conquest of Britain.

Hengest continued his advance inland. His forces now showed no restraint and the massacre that followed set the pattern for the years to come. Soon, in every part of Britain, the barbarians were fighting for power. It was a bitter, merciless fight and some idea of its interminable terror can be imagined from the fact that it took 60 years finally to subdue southern England alone; the conquest was hard won.

In time, areas of occupation began to establish themselves: the Angles were dominant in Northumbria, northern England and the Midlands; the Saxons in East Anglia, Wessex and Sussex; while the Jutes were confined mostly to the area of present-day Kent, where Hengest himself ruled unchallenged until 488.

The invasion and occupation of Britain by the barbarians differed from similar invasions on the continent of Europe, where, on the whole, people continued their way of life and absorbed the conquering newcomers into their society. Britons, however, were driven out of their country or were slaughtered in great numbers, so that over a period of about 150 years Britain became England, literally a land of Englishmen, with a new language, a new religion, new laws and new traditions.

GOOD IDEAS

Stephenson's *Rocket* beat all its rivals.

The steam locomotive has a long history of development. The first person to construct a workable steam engine was Thomas Newcomen, who in the early eighteenth century devised a machine to pump water from mine shafts. Fifty years later James Watt, a Glasgow engineer, improved upon Newcomen's pumps. The resulting machines were very useful in mines and foundries, but Watt was not satisfied. He wanted to produce a steam engine to power a vehicle, and in fact did so with what is still called the 'sun and planets' system of gears.

Another engineer of genius, Richard Trevithick, took Watts' adaptation of the steam engine and put it upon wheels. He built a tiny steam-operated locomotive called Puffing Billy, which he ran as an entertainment in London, but it did not catch public interest sufficiently well.

The era of the railway engine

George Stephenson.

arrived when young George Stephenson persuaded his employer, at Killingworth Colliery on the Tyne, to let him build a steam-powered vehicle to pull trucks of coal from pithead to canal.

In spite of having had little formal education, Stephenson realised that a tremendous future lay with the railways. Whilst others saw them merely as a means of transporting heavy goods, Stephenson realised that they could revolutionise passenger travel. It was lucky that he was a fighting Geordie with a lot of self confidence and a strong sense of humour, for a long and severe struggle lay ahead.

The canal owners opposed him because their trade would suffer, owners of country estates refused to allow railways across their property, and fights took place between estate employees and railway navvies. None of this was good for the image of the new transport, and stories got about, some quite genuinely believed,

which made locomotives seem inventions of the Devil.

Poisoned fumes from engines would kill bird and plant life along the route, sparks would set houses on fire, engine boilers would burst, passengers would go mad as the human frame could not stand motion at more than ten miles an hour . . . there was no end to the tales put about by those who did not want the railways.

But slowly public opinion changed, and Stephenson was allowed to build an official passenger-carrying railway between Manchester and Liverpool. Then the question of finding the best locomotive arose, and in a historic contest at Rainhill, Stephenson's engine the *Rocket* won easily. One competitor's entry was powered by a horse working a kind of treadmill!

The construction of the Manchester and Liverpool railway began a new age in travel. George Stephenson's determined personality brought to fruit the labours of Newcomen, Watt and Trevithick.

THE PROBLEM OF STOPPING

Having got locomotives running successfully, there was still plenty of room for improvement. Railway travel was by no means safe. Then, one day in 1877, a technical magazine came into the hands of a young American engineer, George Westinghouse. When Westinghouse began to read *Living Age* he had a problem on his mind. He was obsessed by the tragedy of frequent railway accidents, having been involved in one himself. Accidents often happened because trains lacked handbrakes of sufficient power to stop heavy engines and coaches quickly.

Pondering this problem, Westinghouse glanced at his magazine, then something caught his attention and he began to pore over an article about compressed-air drills. Compressed air? If this could power drills biting into rock, couldn't it be used to apply a brake?

George Westinghouse.

The young engineer set to work with great energy and soon completed a model of a brake powered by compressed air. The principle was that a handbrake on the engine operated compressed air in pipes which, when pressure was applied, released brake shoes against the locomotive's wheels. Westinghouse knew that it would work but he had to persuade someone to try out his idea.

The big railway companies were not interested. But he possessed the two qualities without which few inventors get very far—faith and persistence. At last he persuaded a railway official to let him experiment with an old engine.

Westinghouse was gambling all he had on the success of his compressed-air brake. He proved the capabilities of his invention in the most dramatic fashion. With his railway friend on board, the engine with its experimental brake was steaming along at forty miles per hour when a horse, cart and driver overturned directly in its path. Normally there would have been little chance of avoiding a collision, but the giant force of the new brake brought the engine to a halt and averted a tragedy.

'That driver is the first of many to owe you his life!' enthused Westinghouse's backer, only slightly less delighted than the inventor himself. Although the brake was not universally accepted immediately, fame and fortune came to Westinghouse at last.

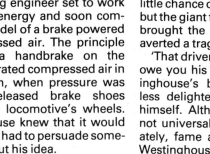

Disaster was averted—thanks to Westinghouse's braking system.

Charles Goodyear.

A LUCKY ACCIDENT

Young Charles Goodyear seemed to suffer from all the bad luck going. His life's ambition was to improve the composition of rubber so that it could be used more widely. It was suitable for weather-proofing clothes and other items, but in hot weather it melted into a foul-smelling gooey mess. In cold weather it became brittle.

Goodyear was convinced that a way existed to 'stabilise' rubber, but he had no sooner interested a wealthy firm in his ideas, than a heatwave ruined their entire stock of merchandise and put Charles out of a job.

The unfortunate young man got into debt and was imprisoned—but like rubber he was tough and resilient and bounced back. Interviewing the prison Governor, he got permission to conduct chemical experiments in his cell.

Out of prison, Goodyear and his wife spent years living from hand to mouth whilst the determined inventor persisted in his efforts. Goodyear's wife hated his smelly experiments, with good reason, and to keep the peace Charles only performed them in her absence.

On her return one day, he hastily threw a piece of unstable rubber, plus some sulphur, into the stove and discovered the answer to his problem by sheer chance! Heat and the action of sulphur transformed the rubber into a firm consistency, resistant to both heat and cold.

Even then Goodyear's troubles were not over, for no-one believed in the breakthrough. He was again imprisoned for unpaid debts. Even after he had proved his process practical, he faced legal difficulties. Worn out by his efforts and by years of struggle, Charles Goodyear died before his success was fully acknowledged. But today the world's largest rubber company bears his name.

Goodyear discovered the answer to his problem—by accident.

These huge rubber tyres are made for use on earth-moving equipment.

A garden hose provided Dunlop's son with a smooth ride.

John Dunlop.

THE SIMPLE SOLUTION

John Dunlop of Belfast was in the garden when his son told him about a bicycle race. The boy complained about the bumpy ride he would have, on a wooden-wheeled bicycle, over the city's cobbled streets, and his father's glance fell upon a garden hose lying nearby. It seemed nothing remarkable to tie the air-filled hose roughly around the back wheels of the bicycle, securing it with cloth. Young Johnny, too excited to wait for the race, tried out the new idea then and there—and it worked. Next day he won the race, and his school friends then wanted similar tyres for their own cycles. Mr Dunlop obliged at first, but the whole thing became troublesome and interfered with his work as a vet. He didn't take his invention seriously: it seemed too simple to be important.

Then a racing cyclist advised him to take out a patent for his air-filled tyre. The vet did so, and found a businessman willing to put it into production. Experts laughed at the innovation.

To Mr Dunlop, his idea was a thing of chance, not something to be defended and persisted in. It was lucky, therefore, that his pneumatic tyres came at a time when the world was ready to accept them. Soon they were fitted to all bicycles and helped to make possible the rapid development of the growing motor car industry. Nowadays the flight of airliners would be impossible without the monster tyres used at takeoff and landing.

The inventor lived to see the principle of his air-filled tyre accepted everywhere. The combination of Goodyear's life's work and Dunlop's momentary inspiration put the petrol-driven vehicle securely in business.

Pneumatic tyres provide cyclists with a smooth comfortable ride.

NEWS THAT TRAVELLED FAST

If Samuel Morse had not sailed from Europe to America in the year 1832, the world might be a different place today. On the month-long voyage, Samuel was given the idea which dominated the rest of his life. It was that of the telegraph, a channel of electric power along which 'instant' signals could be sent.

The notion occupied Morse's mind so totally that he gave up his prosperous career as a portrait painter in order to wrestle with the problem of making a workable channel. It was far from easy, especially as he had had no technical training.

For years Samuel struggled with his do-it-yourself telegraph, opening and closing an electrical circuit which, when closed, attracted a piece of iron with a pencil attached. The pencil would make strokes on paper, according to the length of time the circuit was active. It was all very rough and ready, but it did have the germ of a wonderful invention.

Morse earned his living by teaching art, and he interested a pupil and his father in his ideas. With their help, he constructed a demonstration model of the telegraph. The arrangement of pencil strokes used to carry messages proved too cumbersome, and the trio designed another, based upon the frequency with which letters of the alphabet are used: first E, represented by a dot or very short stroke, and so on. In this way they produced what is today known throughout the world as the Morse Code.

Six years after the idea first occurred to him, Samuel Morse tried to interest the US Government. The difficulties of making the telegraph a practical proposition were nothing compared with those of getting it accepted. The Postal authorities thought of the invention as a rival and conspired to suppress it. Then came success —of a sort! The telegraph line was built, but, at first, no-one wanted to use it. Then news of an important event in Baltimore was immediately telegraphed to Washington, some hundreds of kilometers

Telegraph lines were erected—despite sabotage by farmers who did not want the line across their land.

away, by means of Morse's invention. The news had travelled faster than it would have done by any other method.

Samuel Morse had at last proved his point.

A Morse sounder. This simple yet ingenious device plays an important part in the sending of messages by Morse code.

Guilemo Marconi was determined to see his invention firmly established in the world of communications.

WIRELESS AROUND THE WORLD

The world had to wait some fifty years before another inventor, Guilelmo Marconi, extended Morse's ideas. Instead of telegraph wires, he used electro-magnetic waves for the purpose of transmitting messages. Marconi was lucky in that, although he developed the 'wave' theory himself, the form of his transmission had already been worked out by Morse, and was in constant use.

The Italian inventor was only twenty-two years old when he brought his idea to England. For once authority did not turn a blind eye. The Post Office arranged for Marconi to demonstrate his 'wireless' telegraph across London, and later a tiny telegraph station was set up on the Welsh coast. Because of its great use in communicating with ships at sea, everyone was anxious to find out if the newly-discovered waves could transmit across water. They could. From an island in the Bristol Channel came the signal using the familiar Morse Code. It was the letter V . . . V for Victory!

The success of Marconi's invention was established, but he went on to develop its use. Before he died he saw wireless telegraphy used worldwide, and he put in much of the groundwork for the next step in the communications chain—radio, or to use its formal title, wireless telephony.

Could Marconi's newly-discovered waves travel across water?

88

Good Sports!

Is it possible for a man to set up a world land speed record without travelling on or over any land? The answer is yes! On January 12th, 1904, Henry Ford, founder of the Ford motor industry, drove his Arrow racing car at the previously unattained speed of 91.37 m.p.h.—over the frozen surface of Lake St. Clair near Detroit!

There was only one runner in the final of the 440 yards race in the 1908 Olympic Games, held in London. It was, in fact, a re-run of the original final, in which three Americans, Carpenter, Robbins and Taylor, had been accused of obstructing the fourth finalist, British Wyndham Halswelle. The Americans, who objected to the decision, refused to take part in the re-run. So Halswelle ran alone to receive the winner's gold medal.

One of the most remarkable speed records ever set by man was that of 614 m.p.h. This record was made without any mechanical aid. When you consider that a world-class sprinter is capable of running no faster than approximately 23 m.p.h. you may think that 614 m.p.h. belongs to the world of fantasy. Nevertheless this is the speed that was attained in a sky-diving drop in the rarefied atmosphere of high altitudes.

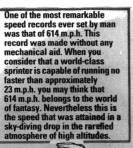

Before the Amateur Athletics Association was formed in 1880, professional foot-racing, or pedestrianism, was a very popular sport. No less than 25,000 spectators attended a pedestrian meeting at Powderhall, near Edinburgh, in 1869. One of the events was a sixty-hour race in which the winner covered just over 352 miles.

The tug-of-war must be one of the slowest events on record. Two well-matched teams can take a long time to settle a contest. Such was the pull at Juppalpore, India, on August 12th, 1889, between teams from the British Army. The winning team took 2 hours 41 minutes to move a distance of 12 feet! This works out at an average speed of 0.0008 miles per hour.

THE STORY OF MILLING

The earliest known form of milling began by man crushing grain between two flat stones. He soon discovered it was more effective to pound the grain, holding a small round stone in one hand with the grain lying on a flat rock. With use, the flat rock would have formed a hollow and together with the small rock, would have become man's first primitive pestle and mortar. The earliest known example of a pestle and mortar is over five thousand years old. Illustrations on Egyptian tomb paintings and Greek vases show them being used to grind corn.

The people of ancient Egypt and Babylon soon found that lifting a stone to pound grain was hard work, and instead a rubbing action could be used, as in the case of the saddlestone mill. This had a sloping lower half, called the millstone, on which grain was rubbed using a grindstone shaped like a rolling pin. The miller would kneel behind the millstone, pushing the grindstone up and down the slope. This was still hard work, and not very productive. Working full-time, this method could only provide sufficient flour for eight people.

A big step forward was made by the introduction of the rotary mill which produced a continuous rubbing action. Large quantities of grain could now be ground on a commercial scale. The millers of ancient Greece and Rome used rotary mills shaped like big hour glasses. Twenty such mill-bakeries have been found in the ruins of Pompeii, each one producing enough bread to feed one thousand people. Efficient milling was very important for the Romans since they introduced a free bread ration as an early form of dole.

The quern was a smaller version of the rotary mill, developed for use in the home. It probably first appeared in the Near East, and was in use in Britain about two thousand years ago. A carefully operated quern could produce finer flour than the hour glass mill and was probably twelve times as productive as the saddlestone mill.

As long as mills were turned by men, or even animals, their size and capacity were limited. With the harnessing of water power to drive the millstones, milling took another big step forward. The earliest type of watermill was built by the Norsemen with the wheel laid horizontally in the stream. The shaft driving the millstones was vertical, with one end resting on the bed of the stream. The Romans introduced the vertically mounted water wheel, using a system of gears to produce the vertical motion required by the millstones. They first introduced the watermill to England and hundreds of them were found in operation by the Normans.

While watermills were ideal in wet hilly country with plenty of running water, the windmill was first developed where it was both flat and dry. The first windmills were found about one thousand years ago, in what is now part of Eastern Iran. Here the wind blows constantly for nine months of the year, and always from the same direction. These windmills used hrizontally mounted sails like the Norse watermill. The origin of the vertical sail mill is uncertain, but they were operating in England by the 11th century. Such mills could drive millstones of up to 3¼ metres in diameter and weighing 1780 kilograms. The best stone came from Burr in the Paris basin, and although it is still used today, nearly all milling is now done by chilled cast iron rollers.

The modern roller mill, with its cast iron rollers, was first used in Hungary and Switzerland between 1870 and 1885. The cast iron rollers gave greater control than the old millstones and were cheaper to use. Grooved iron rollers turn the grain into three elements: bran, middlings and semolina. These elements are then sifted on silk or nylon sieves. The bran, which is formed from the outer husk of the wheat, goes principally to make cattle feed, while the middlings and semolina are passed through smooth iron rollers. After twelve or thirteen separate stages of grinding and sifting, the middlings and semolina are finally turned into flour. Like most modern industrial processes, the flour mill is highly automated.

SHIPWRECK!

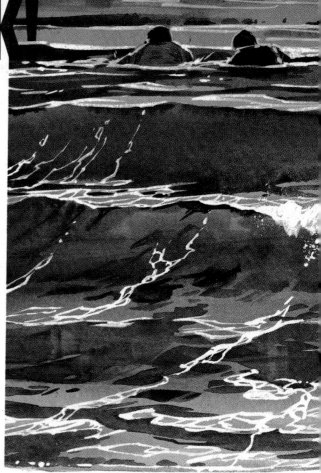

Exactly two months to the day since she had left Melbourne, Australia, the iron ship *Royal Charter* rounded The Skerries, a lonely outcrop of rocks lying just off the north-west tip of the Isle of Anglesey. Though her single screw was driven by an engine of no more than 200 horse-power and she was of 2,719 tons displacement, she had made remarkable time. In fact, her passengers were so pleased with the swift passage that they had drawn up a testimonial of their esteem for the master of the ship, Captain Taylor, and collected sufficient money among themselves to be able to make a presentation to him on arrival at Liverpool, their destination.

A foolhardy captain might have tried to save time on the last short lap of the voyage by steaming between The Skerries and Carmel Head. But not Captain Taylor: he was a veteran employee of the company Gibb & Bright of Liverpool, who owned the vessel, and was not a man to take risks. What is more, as the ship swung eastwards beyond The Skerries he realized that this final lap, of some 60 sea-miles, would be in the teeth of an east-north-easterly gale. But his 200-h.p. engine was functioning well and he still had plenty of coal in his bunkers. He would give the north coast of Anglesey a wide berth, raise all the steam he could in his boilers, and with luck tie up in Liverpool Docks inside eight hours, or ten hours at most.

The *Royal Charter* had a crew of 112 officers and men. She carried a valuable cargo, which included nearly 80,000 ounces of pure Australian gold. She had cabin and deck accommodation for almost 400 passengers. In all, there were 498 men, women and children on board. Of these, when that terrible night was out, only 39 escaped with their lives, and many of those were badly injured.

The lighthouse on Point Lynas, on the north-eastern tip of Anglesey, hove into view before midnight on the evening of Tuesday, 25th October, 1859. Captain Taylor remarked that he was closer to it than he cared to be, and promptly ordered the helmsman to alter course a few points to port. Soon afterwards the helmsman protested that he could not hold the course laid down for him because the gale on his port beam was so strong, and even increasing in strength.

It was a pitch dark night: no moon, not a star in the sky. The only light was that of the Lynas Point lighthouse—and that was now all too close for comfort. As a precaution, Captain Taylor gave orders for signal-rockets

Captain Taylor of the 'Royal Charter' should have received a testimonial from his passengers for their swift trip from Australia. As it turned out, he and nearly everyone else on board perished a few miles from their journey's end. Only a few survivors staggered ashore.

to be fired and blue lights to be shown. At the same time he decided to run for shelter, if possible, in Dulas Bay, even though that meant being dangerously close to a lee shore.

In the bay he dropped anchor both fore and aft, but kept his engine running to ease the strain on the anchor-chains. As they began to drag, he adopted the desperate expedient of cutting down his masts to lessen the wind-resistance. Unluckily, the rigging from one mast fouled the screw when it tumbled overboard and the screw ground to a halt. Now the *Royal Charter* was completely helpless, at the mercy of both the on-shore gale and the irresistible set of the tide towards the rocks.

One of the few survivors put on record what happened from that point onwards: "Having such confidence in Captain Taylor," he wrote, "I had gone to my cabin. Suddenly I heard a voice cry out: 'Come directly, we are all lost!' It was the voice of a fellow-passenger, a Captain Withers, who had himself once suffered shipwreck. By my watch it was three o'clock in the morning. Hastily throwing on a few articles of attire, I ran up on deck. I found the ship was drifting towards some rocks, and at that very moment she was thrown upon them and we all fell to the deck at the sudden impact. Our ship bumped heavily two or three times more. All was confusion,

families clung to one another, the younger children crying out piteously.

"Just then a huge wave came down upon the ship with tremendous force, breaking through the skylights and hatches. The ship bumped on the rocks continuously for two hours and more, and the seas rushed in with ever-increasing force. I, with many others, was knocked by the waves against the wall of the saloon as we tried to make our way up on deck, having no wish to be drowned below like rats in a sinking ship—as indeed we were."

"Soon afterwards, a great sea came against us broadside and broke the ship quite in two, just at the engine-room. The two halves of the ship then slewed round, and each became a total wreck. Parties of men, women and children, passengers and crew alike, were carried down with the debris, and as many must have been killed as drowned. Having made up my mind that I had best jump overboard into the sea on the lee side, I attempted to lay hold of a rope. But instead I fell headlong into deep water, which was so thickly strewn with portions of the wreck that I had to force an opening with my arms before I could come to the surface. I was repeatedly thrown ashore, and as often washed back. But at last some seamen who had reached shore managed to grasp my outstretched hands and so rescue me. By that time I was insensible."

his gallant effort failed.

As the first streaks of light broke over Dulas Bay, they floodlit a terrible scene. The ship had wholly disintegrated. Tossing about in the raging sea were the bodies of men, women and children. Trunks and chests and personal possessions tossed on the water, breaking up on impact with the wreckage and the lurking rocks, whose tips only just projected through the water now that the tide was near full. Though she had been an iron ship, all that was left of her consisted of a few contorted metal sheets. Many of the casualties owed their terrible injuries to having been thrown against them by the surge of the waves and cut to pieces.

When daylight had fully come, rescue parties had reached the bay, summoned by the first men to struggle ashore and survive the ordeal. But they came too late.

Theirs was now the grisly task of collecting, over succeeding days, no fewer than 459 bodies. They were assisted by the able-bodied among 39 passengers and crew, almost equal in numbers. Veteran Captain Taylor, of the *Royal Charter,* for whom the testimonial and gift had been planned by his grateful passengers for presentation on arrival at Liverpool, was not among them: he had gone down with his ship.

This fortunate survivor did not know of the gallant attempt made, strangely enough, by a Portuguese sailor as soon as the ship went aground. Unlike most seamen in those days, he was a strong swimmer, and he offered to take a line ashore and make it fast so that he could then haul a heavier rope ashore, so that this lifeline would enable some, if not all, of those on board to make their way to safety. He did in fact reach the shore, miraculously escaping being smashed to pieces on the rocks. But the line was too short, and was snatched from his hand before he could make it fast, so

93

NEW ROOFS FOR OLD

A simple, beautiful example of long straw thatching, with decoration along the ridge of the roof and two small upper windows with their characteristic 'eyebrows' of thatch.

Today we all of us live in "The Machine Age", an age of assembly-lines and mass-production, automation, computerisation. Only elderly people can remember when every community had its own group of craftsmen, each one skilled in a special craft, and all working with simple raw materials—reed and straw, oak and ash, elm and hazel, rush and osiers: growing materials, all of them. There is little demand today for those fine craftsmen. The old-fashioned wheelwright (who worked in oak, ash and elm) has gone; the wagon-wheel he so skilfully built is today a pressed-steel disc with a pneumatic tyre. The old-fashioned smithy, which was often next door to the wheel-wright, is now a garage, or a service-station for tractors and com-bine-harvesters.

Still, some country crafts have survived. One of these is that of the thatcher, who works in a tradition thousands of years old. Man's earliest home, after he had moved out of the cave, was covered, as it was built, by materials lying readily to hand. He used turf, ling (heather), brushwood: all excellently weather-proof as well as cheap or free. Then he turned to wheat-straw and reed.

The thatchers of today prefer reed as found in East Anglia and Somerset. A good reed thatch will last a hundred years, though it is expensive compared with straw thatch, which will last about half that time.

Thatchers are highly skilled craftsmen. A thatcher often inherits his skill, as well as his simple but efficient equipment, from his father and forefathers. His sheep-shears, bone-handled knife, 'needle' and 'shingling-hammer' may have been made by the local blacksmith, though he will have made the rest of his tackle himself. Most important, save perhaps for the shears, is the 'beetle'. This is a heavy, grooved wooden board with a short handle, used to hammer the butt-ends of each 'thrave', or bundle, of reed or straw, so that the tapering ends are driven well home into the butt-ends of the thrave above.

He uses a home-made 'comb' to unravel any tangles, and a huge 'needle' and tarred string to 'sew' the thraves to the battens below. Or he may fasten them down with rows of hazel 'twists', like giant hairpins, known to thatchers in different parts of the country as 'spars', 'roovers', 'sparrods', 'brotches', 'spics', 'tangs', 'splints' and —the best name of all, perhaps—'withynecks'. To carry his thraves up the ladder he uses a 'carrier', shaped like a wooden-pronged pitchfork, with a noose to hold the straw between the prongs.

Watch any thatcher at work and you will see that he never hurries, never makes a false move. He works from right to left and, like the tile-layer, from the eaves upwards. Every move is calculated. He rarely uses tape or measuring-rod, even for the complicated thatching of gable-ends and dormer-windows. He works, as his forefathers before him worked, by eye alone; and his eye is as quick and accurate as that of any spin-bowler, fencer or billiards-player. The roof of thatch seems to 'grow' beneath his expert touch. And this is not really surprising, for he is working with what was, until only a short while before, a living and growing material: straw from a harvested wheatfield or reed from the shallow waterways of East Anglia or Somerset. Soon the building—whether house or farmhouse, tractor-shed or barn—will be roofed with a shimmering cover of what looks almost like molten gold.

Thatchers, by tradition, are artists as well as craftsmen. They are rarely content simply to construct a roof out of reed or straw. No, the thatch must be made ornamental; it must be given a pattern; it must present something of a picture, quite apart from the natural glossy beauty of the material from which it is made. The pattern he gives it will vary from one part of the country to another, even from one district or parish to another, according to the tradition of the thatcher's family which he is carrying on. The most notable patterning will always be found along the ridge of the roof between the gable-ends.

Here the tapering ends of the uppermost row of thraves will have been turned over from opposite sides, like clasped fingers, and interlocked to make the ridge completely watertight. The thatcher takes a good supply of hazel twists and a number of lengths of straight hazels, known as 'ledgers'. He lays these parallel with the ridge and links them with short-cut ledgers, set diagonally across one another to form a diamond pattern, the corners of the diamonds being held down on the thatch by the twists.

In addition to forming patterns with his lengths of hazel, and sometimes even with brambles, he can pattern the actual thatch by cutting it. Thatch above the eaves is usually left dead straight, though sometimes it is 'scalloped'. But a foot or two below the ridge, and over gable-ends and dormer-windows, he may trim the butt-ends of the thatch into alternating 'tongues', long and short, or into

A Norfolk reed thatcher with some of his raw material, six carefully graded and tied bunches of reed, ready to be taken up the ladder to the roof.

A Norfolk reed thatcher puts the finishing touches to his work with a long-bladed trimming knife. The interlaced decorative diamond pattern is made of split hazel branches.

'dog-tooth' patterns. The smaller windows give him the opportunity to form what at a distance looks uncommonly like eyebrows, especially when they are set in the snug roof of a small cottage.

It is this individual style of thatching, and in ornamenting the thatch, that serves as the 'hall-mark' of the thatcher. Most of them are old, or at least elderly men, today; but happily you may occasionally still come across a young man, sometimes little more than a lad, who has decided that he would rather spend his life working with 'natural' materials than be just a unit on an assembly-line, churning out mechanical bits-and-pieces that never could possess the hall-mark of individuality that is always the well-marked feature of a reed- or straw-thatched roof.

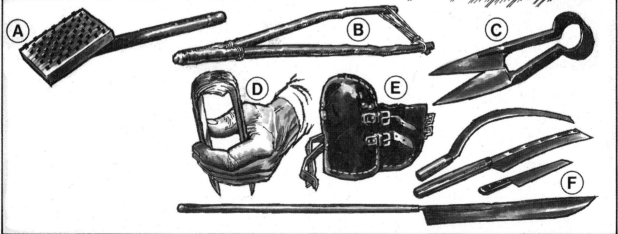

THE TOOLS OF A CRAFTSMAN

The large illustration (above right) shows a Norfolk reed thatcher at work. With the hammer, he is driving home an iron spike. Stuck in the thatch beside him are two of the many types and sizes of stitching and reeding needles he uses. The other tools shown here, not to scale, are A a Norfolk reed 'leggett', used for dressing the reed into position, B a carrying yoke for bunches or 'yealms' of long straw, C trimming shears, D a hazel 'twist' or 'spar', the giant 'hairpin' made from split hazel branches used in fixing the thatch in position, E protective knee-pads and F trimming knives of various sizes and uses.

THE 'FISH' THAT ISN'T~THAT'S

By tradition, most members of the whale family (together with the sturgeon) are called "Royal Fish" and belong to the Crown. This means that when, for instance, a whale is found stranded on a beach, it usually has to be reported to the British Museum, which uses the information to plot the movements of the different species.

Of course whales are not fish—they are mammals of the sea. Many people think of them as rare animals, and this is true of those which have been hunted almost to extinction. Fortunately, there is a move among certain countries of the world to control whaling and with luck the threatened species will survive, at least for a few more generations.

Many species of whales and dolphins (which are really small members of the whale families) are not rare, but unless you spend a great deal of time at sea or live near the coast, you are unlikely to see them.

Dolphins have become better known to the general public since the discovery was made in Florida that they could be kept in captivity. The high intelligence of the whole family has now been proved beyond doubt by American scientists.

The lesser rorqual (Balaenoptera acutorostrata) is small when compared to many whales, rarely growing to more than 9 metres long. These whales are not very common in northern waters, although they do sometimes turn up in unusual places. Only a few years ago one swam up the River Thames as far as Kew Bridge.

Like other baleen whales, this species feeds almost entirely on near-microscopic animals known as krill.

A few whales of the Ziphius cavirostris species, known as Cuvier's beaked whale, have been found on British beaches, but generally this is a semi-tropical species which prefers warm waters. It grows to about 7.5 metres.

The bottle-nosed whale (Hyperoodon ampullatus) is a strange-looking animal with a bulging forehead (often described as a melon). It grows up to 9 metres long.

The blackfish or pilot whale (Globicephala melaena) can grow to more than 6 metres long. It also has a melon-shaped forehead but a shorter "beak" than the bottle-nosed whale. It is common along Scottish coasts.

Growing up to 9 metres long, the killer whale (Orcinus orca) is also called the grampus. This is an attractive black and white animal with a distinctive high dorsal fin. A ferocious beast, it kills seals and seabirds for food—and has even been known to tip up boats in order to eat the occupants!

The sei whale (Balaenoptera borealis) is one of the rorqual group of whales. It grows to about 18 metres long and is rarely found round British coasts.

The small white-beaked dolphin (Lagenorhynchus albirostris) grows to 3 metres long. It lives in schools of up to 100 animals.

The common dolphin (Delphinus delphis) generally grows to about 2 metres long. It is probably the second most common of all the whales around our coasts.

The most common member of the whale family found in British waters is undoubtedly its smallest member—the porpoise (Phocaena phocaena). Shoals of about fifty of these little animals are often seen offshore by anglers and swimmers.

Porpoises tend to be less tolerant of human beings than many other species, and are rarely kept in captivity.

The bottle-nosed dolphin (Tursiops truncatus), which grows to about 3.5 metres long, has proved itself to be not only highly intelligent, but also the clown of the sea. It seems to enjoy amusing crowds of onlookers.

Risso's dolphin (Grampus griseus) is only a little larger than the bottle-nosed dolphin, but it does not have the long snout.

A really big whale, growing to 24 metres long or more, is the fin whale or common rorqual (Balaenoptera physalus). This is found in almost all the seas of the world.

The white-sided dolphin (Lagenorhynchus acutus) is considered fairly common in northern British waters. These animals, which are among the most attractive members of the whale family, move around in large shoals hunting for fish.

Feeding time at a Dolphinarium in the USA.

THE WHALE

THE WORLD'S HOTTEST, DEADLIEST VALLEY

Scotty's grave overlooking Death Valley.

An old trailer used in the borax mines.

The old-timers came this way in search of gold and silver. They found nothing but a natural furnace—and left behind a legend

Death Valley, California, is 100 kilometres long, flanked by forbidding mountains and as fearsome a place as you can imagine on a day when the temperature leaps into the 120s Fahrenheit.

Strangely, although its awesome silence is one of the first things that strikes the visitor, Death Valley has always acted as something of a magnet to human beings. For a thousand years Shoshone Indians lived there, learning where to find water underground and how to survive on the sparse desert vegetation.

In the mid-nineteenth century, the shy and isolated Shoshone, who must have felt very safe from all enemies in their harsh environment, hid behind dwarf bushes and watched as pioneers from the East—white men in search of new lands—drifted away from the main tide of westward migration and "discovered" and named Death Valley.

As the white pioneers struck its northern end they must have thought that the way ahead looked flat and

Above: Smooth drifts of sand and harsh mountains form part of the many different kinds of terrain seen in Death Valley. Here the temperature often exceeds 120 degrees Fahrenheit.

Left: Scotty's Castle, built by a mining engineer as his retreat and now an attraction for tourists. To provide fuel for his power plant, the owner bought up a stock of old railway sleepers sufficient to last for 80 years.

easy. Then, as they advanced along the valley floor, they found that it was baking hot, very rocky and very grim.

But when silver was later discovered in a neighbouring valley, prospectors flocked into Death Valley to see if there was more. There wasn't, and legend says that the valley's intense heat claimed many victims.

DISCOVERY

That didn't seem to worry Aaron Winters, who lived with his wife Rose at Ash Meadows in the neighbouring State of Nevada. Aaron and Rose were camping under the lee of Funeral Mountains, on the valley's edge, when they discovered not silver but borax—the "white gold of the desert".

Borax is chemically the acid borate of sodium. When it is fused a transparent glass is obtained, which can be coloured in different ways by various metallic oxides. It is also much used as a detergent, as a flux for metals, in calico-printing and as a solvent in making glazing compounds.

Aaron Winters knew what he was looking for when he made camp, and a romantic tale of his discovery was later told in a book about the valley. We are told that as night fell Winters and his wife had only "the faint glow of a few dying coals" for light.

They sat down on the sand, put a saucer of the material they had gathered on the rock between them, poured some chemicals and alcohol over it, and then Winters scratched a match to set the mixture alight. "He held the blaze to the mixture in the saucer with a trembling hand and then shouted at the top of his voice: 'She burns green, Rosie! We're rich!'"

MULE TRAIN

The problem, though, was how to get the borax out of Death Valley. In that fearful heat, a road was constructed from Furnace Creek, in the centre of the valley, to Mojave, 265 kilometres away. Along this road teams of mules, 16, 18 and 20 strong, pulled trailers containing 36-ton loads. The trip to Mojave took 12 days of torment, at the end of which there were some rich prospectors and some tired mules.

The weather is a constantly fascinating subject in Death Valley. The average rainfall there is under four centimetres a year—land is defined as desert if it gets less than 25.5 centimetres of rain a year.

Summertime temperatures often exceed 120 degrees Fahrenheit, and 134 degrees in the shade has been recorded. At night in summer the temperature rarely falls below 85 degrees.

But there are often tremendous

Visitors waiting to do the tour of Scotty's Castle.

Twisted deadwood makes a grotesque shape in the valley's sand dunes.

Far left: Monument to "Death Valley Scotty." The inscription, prepared by Scotty himself, reads: "I got four things to live by. Don't say nothing that will hurt anybody. Don't give advice—nobody will take it anyway. Don't complain. Don't explain." Above: The magnificent sitting room of Scotty Castle.

Left: The courtyard inside the Castle. The bridge connects the main rooms on the right with the guests' section.

variations of temperature between the valley floor and the peaks that dot the valley—sometimes the temperature difference can be as much as 50 degrees.

A good deal of the floor of the valley is covered with a thin layer of salt which, seen from a distance, looks like sheets of water shimmering in the sun. And, indeed, it was once water. Many centuries ago Death Valley was a salt lake that gradually evaporated, leaving behind its mineral content.

A visitor to the valley can spend several days there and still be struck by the utter barrenness of the place. A longer stay and closer inspection reveals that the desert is very much

alive. Insects crawl between the shreds of thin foliage. A type of rattlesnake called a sidewinder, because of its sideways movement, sidles across the smooth sand crests.

About 600 different kinds of plants —most of them small, some of them tiny—grow in the valley. The mesquite bean bush provides food for birds and coyotes—once it also provided the staple diet of the Shoshone Indians—and other plants provide food for darting lizards.

Among all this life there are small herds of shy desert bighorn sheep, forever roaming as they chew at the sparse vegetation. Fortunately, they, require little water, getting most of

their liquid needs from the plants they eat.

Occasionally a burro and his mate can be seen standing stockstill on a hillside. A burro is a descendant from the donkeys that worked in the old borax mines and which were turned loose by the workmen when the mines periodically failed. They have grown used to their harsh environment but they are still alien to it, for they upset the delicate balance of nature by eating too much of the vegetation.

Apart from his mistake with the burros, man has generally treated Death Valley, now a national park, with respect and admiration. Only a couple of roads cross the valley. One

Left: Lovely desert flowers bring a variety of summertime colours to the valley, softening its barren face.

Below: Wild burros, decendants from the miners'donkeys, roam the parts of the valley where sparse vegetation grows.

Another strange variety of terrain found in the valley. This area is called the Devil's Cornfield.

of them leads to a motel with a swimming pool, built on a green and welcoming oasis, but the traveller in Death Valley has great need of such a haven.

Undoubtedly, the valley's most fascinating story centres on its only other noteworthy building, Scotty's Castle. It concerns two very different men who met and formed an extraordinary partnership.

Albert Johnson was a mining engineer and businessman who, early in the twentieth century, had made himself a multi-million dollar fortune. Well-educated and financially shrewd, he had been brought up a strict Quaker.

In contrast, Walter Scott had received little formal education, and in his teens earned a meagre living as a cowhand. In 1890, his talents as a horseman got him a job in the Buffalo Bill Wild West Show. Scott loved the limelight, and the show allowed him to develop his special brand of dry wise-cracking humour that was to endear him to the serious, reserved Johnson, when eventually they met.

In 1905, Scott walked into a New York bank with two souvenir gold nuggets he had obtained from a gold mine in Colorado and claimed that he had discovered gold in Death Valley, California. On the strength of the two nuggets, the bank advanced him a considerable sum in cash to develop his "mine". Scotty, as he was called, at once set about spending the money freely, all the time claiming that this wealth was the proceeds of his Death Valley gold mine.

DESERT HOME

By the time it was discovered that there was no mine and that Scotty was a hoaxer, he had not only become an American legend, but had met mining engineer Albert Johnson. One day, Scotty took Johnson to Death Valley (though not to his "mine", of course) and the mining engineer fell in love with the place. Here, he decided with Scotty's enthusiastic backing, he would build a magnificent desert home, miles from anywhere.

As the vast, one-and-a-half million dollar building developed, the American Press became deeply intrigued. Why should anyone want to build such a palatial-style residence in the middle of nowhere, scorched by the sun all the year round? For all

their questions Scotty, now Johnson's inseparable companion, had a ready answer. "It's just my summer shack," he would say with a shrug. The Press preferred to call it a castle. Because Scotty was always on hand and Johnson tended to stay in the background they then dubbed it Scotty's Castle— and Johnson didn't seem to mind in the least.

The "castle" is a Spanish-type mansion equipped with all manner of 1920s gadgetry—like a vast 1,000-pipe electric organ in the music room which plays automatically at the touch of a button. One can imagine the thunderous sound wafting out of the "castle" into the total silence of Death Valley—a trick still demonstrated by guides for tourists who visit Scotty's Castle.

Albert Johnson lost most of his fortune in the 1929 Wall Street Stock Market crash and retired permanently to Scotty's Castle, where he died. The huge swimming pool was still unfinished and remains so to this day, but Scotty lived on there alone. He died in 1954, and was buried on a small hill by the house in the valley that had helped to make him a part of American folklore.

A HOLE FOR A HOME

R.B.Davis

The "laughing" call of the green wood-pecker, the largest of Britain's three native woodpeckers, is a familiar sound in many of our woods and forests. Like all wood-peckers, this bird has strong hooked claws so it can cling to the bark of a tree while searching for the grubs and insects which hide in the crevices.

It makes its home in a tree by chipping a hole in the trunk with its sharp beak. The hole is about eight centimetres across, and goes into the trunk a little way before turning downwards and opening out into a chamber where the eggs are laid and the young reared.

103

The diary kept by James Boswell presented the world with a fascinating portrait of one of Britain's greatest literary geniuses

The most famous of all literary friendships is the one between Dr. Samuel Johnson and the Scottish writer James Boswell. It is doubtful how much of Johnson's writing and reputation would have survived the centuries if Boswell had not composed "the greatest biography written in English"—his *Life Of Samuel Johnson*.

For years the two men were constant companions. They ate, drank, and journeyed together, exchanging ideas and discussing every subject under the sun. And always, as the pearls of wit and wisdom dropped from Johnson's lips, Boswell was there to gather them up.

It is thanks to Boswell that we can today enjoy such of Johnson's sayings as: "It matters not how a man dies, but how he lives. The act of dying is not of importance, it lasts so short a time" . . . "Patriotism is the last refuge of a scoundrel" . . . "No man but a blockhead ever wrote, except for money" . . . "When a man is tired of London, he is tired of life" . . . "Every man thinks meanly of himself for not having been a soldier, or not having been at sea."

LACK OF MONEY

Johnson was born in 1709, at Lichfield, Staffs, the son of a bookseller. He received his early education in his home town, and later went to Pembroke College, Oxford, where lack of money made him leave before taking a degree. Some years of poverty and struggle followed, during which he was first a school teacher and then worked for a publisher in Birmingham.

Then, in 1735, the year he anonymously translated a book called *Voyage To Abyssinia*, written by a Portuguese missionary, he married a widow named Elizabeth Porter. Although she was twenty years older than Johnson, he was genuinely attached to her—and was also grateful for the £800 she possessed.

He next opened—and quickly closed—a boys' school at Edial, near Lichfield. He enrolled only three pupils, one of them the eighteen-year-old David Garrick who was destined to become one of Britain's greatest Shakespearean actors. Johnson was quick to spot the young man's budding genius, and is reputed to have told Garrick's mother that "David will either be hanged, or become a great man."

Together with Garrick, Johnson moved to London, where, after some

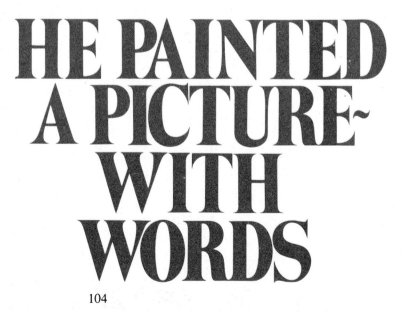

HE PAINTED A PICTURE- WITH WORDS

As usual, the meeting of the Literary Club was dominated by the pock-scarred man—Dr Samuel Johnson—a writer and brilliant conversationalist.

From Boswell we learn of Johnson's kindness and generosity. When going home to his Fleet Street rooms late at night, he often passed poor children asleep in doorways, and always put money in their hands.

years spent working as a journalist, poet, and unsuccessful playwright, he published in 1755 his famous *Dictionary Of The English Language*. He said the book was "written with little assistance of the learned, and without any patronage of the great . . . amid inconvenience and distraction, in sickness and in sorrow."

CHANGE OF FORTUNE

In 1762, fortune turned in Johnson's favour. He was awarded a state pension of £300, and the following year he made the acquaintance of Boswell.

When Johnson died in 1784, he was buried in Westminster Abbey, and a statue of him was erected in St. Paul's. He lives on, not so much through his writing as through Boswell's marvellous description of him. And it is easy for us to picture the doctor with his bushy wig, deep voice, poor eyesight, jerky movements, and large clumsy body.

Johnson was at his greatest whilst talking, and is better appreciated in Boswell's incomparable biography than in any books or essays of his own.

xIn 1773, Boswell persuaded the great literary lion of London to accompany him on a tour of the Western Islands of Scotland. Johnson was then 64, more than twenty years older than his companion, but he followed Boswell courageously wherever he went, often sleeping in nothing better than a barn.

Boswell eventually became the recorder for Carlisle, before his death in 1795. In those intervening years, he was often to recall fondly all the happy days he had spent with Johnson—particularly when they had visited the Hebrides.

CAT FROM A COLD CLIMATE

Still almost unknown and unmapped, the high plateau of Tibet provides a harsh, inhospitable home for the many creatures that live there. The climate is like that of the Arctic tundra, although the hot plains of India lie just to the south.

As darkness descends over the cold, desolate uplands, the most beautiful of the world's mountain-dwellers leaves it home to begin its nocturnal prowl in search of prey.

This is the snow leopard, a formidable predator which haunts the heights of the mighty Himalayas, where freezing winds rage across the bleak land and where, even in summertime, severe frosts chill the night air.

The rare snow leopard, or ounce, as it is sometimes called, goes where its food is to be found. Midsummer finds it roaming among the mountain heights, over 5,000 metres above sea level. The bitter, cold winds of winter then force it back to as low as 1,800 metres as it continues its search for wild sheep, ibex, musk deer and small rodents. For when these creatures make their seasonal migrations, the snow leopard follows them.

Like the tiger, the lion and the puma, the snow leopard belongs to the great Cat family, but though it is similar in size and appearance, it is not just a mountain race of the true leopard. It is a quite separate species and is found only in Central Asia.

It has many characteristics in common with all its relatives, however, for it is a wonderfully agile, lithe hunter with a keen sense of hearing and smell. But compared with the true leopard, the snow leopard is a much more placid, less savage animal.

As an example of the perfect snow predator, the snow leopard stands supreme. It has a heavily furred coat which protects it against the rigorous climate of its home.

The deep soft fur is pale grey or creamy buff in colour and the patches on its body provide a perfect camouflage to make the animal look like the snowy rocks among which it hunts. It has an enormous tail which is longer than the head and body together. This acts as a counterpoise, as the cat needs careful balance when climbing trees, springing on prey, or moving over the steep slopes. Like the body, the tail is covered with thick fur to prevent heat loss.

But the most distinctive feature of its appearance is the superb coat of fur, beautifully marked with dark rosettes on the back and flanks.

The snow leopard's coat is one of the most highly prized in the fur markets of the world, and as a result, this species has suffered widespread persecution over the years.

Experts estimate that only 400 of these creatures remain in the whole Himalayan complex.

TENNIS
A Sport
Of
Kings

Tennis is one of the world's great international sports, played from Argentina to Korea, from Iceland to Polynesia, on surfaces ranging from baked mud to rich lawn. At one time it was a reasonably gentle game; today it calls for power and stamina as well as skill.

When we talk about tennis these days, we most likely have "lawn tennis" in mind, the game invented in 1874 by Major Walter Clopton Wingfield, who patented it under the name "Sphairistiké", which comes from a Greek word meaning "playing at ball". Not surprisingly, this tongue-twister had a very short life.

Not so the game! It was quickly adopted by the Marylebone Cricket Club, who drew up the first set of rules in 1875, but it was left to the All England Croquet Club at Wimbledon to get the sport really off the ground. They quickly added "Lawn Tennis" to their name, modified and added to the MCC rules, and by 1877 they were able to stage the first British lawn tennis championships on a grass court which they had lost no time in preparing. The first "Wimbledon" had 22 competitors.

Lawn tennis, however, goes back much further than the days of Major Wingfield. It had its roots in "jeu de paume", a game played in the monasteries of France as early as the 10th century. As there were no rackets in those days, the ball was struck with the palm of the hand—hence the name.

Later, this primitive pastime developed into tennis proper (also called court tennis, royal tennis or real tennis). It flourished to such an extent in France that by 1596 there were 250 real tennis courts in Paris alone. The game also became popular in England under the patronage of Henry VII and Henry VIII, who ordered the real tennis court, at Hampton Court Palace, to be built.

Real tennis survives today, but precariously. From its former eminence there remain only two courts in France, two in Australia, one in Scotland, six in the USA and 15 in England.

However, its first cousin has never looked back. By 1900, lawn tennis was making rapid strides not only in Britain and the USA but also in Europe, South Africa and Australia. In 1883, the famous tennis brothers, W. and E. Renshaw, met the Ameri-

Tennis has always been a popular sport with women. The dresses worn by these players, seen taking part in a doubles match in 1877, must have hampered them somewhat!

Suzanne Lenglen was one of the greatest women tennis players of all time. In 1925 she won the Wimbledon Ladies' Singles Championship, losing only five games during the whole tournament.

The first match played between Britain and America for the Davis Cup was played in 1900. The Americans won and the man who thought up the idea for the contest, Dwight Davis (in the centre of the picture), was a member of the winning team.

The Centre Court at Wimbledon has seen many great players since it was opened in 1922 by King George V.

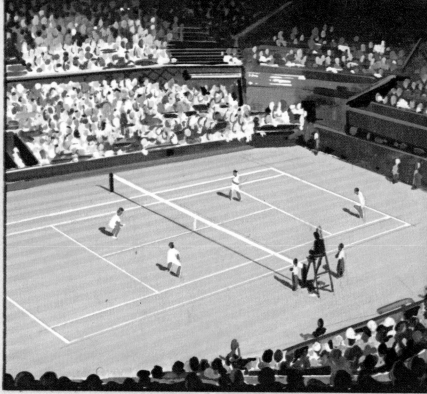

can brothers, C. M. and J. S. Clark, at Wimbledon, where they won the first international tennis contest.

Women, too, were very much involved in the game. They held their first championships at Wimbledon in 1884, and in 1887 their American sisters staged theirs at Philadelphia.

Tennis made a fitting start to the twentieth century with the introduction of the Davis Cup, a trophy presented by Dwight D. Davis, a student at Harvard University. This has since become the great team event of tennis and, unofficially, it decides which is to be the champion nation. More than 60 countries have competed since the USA and Britain met in the first match at a cricket club, near Boston in 1900, but only four have ever won the Cup: Australia, the USA, Britain and France.

Players such as the Renshaw brothers and the Doherty brothers were able to win the Wimbledon championships year after year, partly through ability and partly through the lack of competition.

The game still lacked most of the power and ruthlessness of today. Indeed, the cannon−ball service, introduced by an American, Maurice McLoughlin, did not evolve until 1912. From then until quite recently play was dominated from the base line, among the greatest exponents of this strategy being Big Bill Tilden, whom some rate as the most complete player ever.

It is a bold claim, for, in common with other sports, tennis techniques have been steadily developing over the years. How then would he have shaped against the explosive brilli-ance of men like Jimmy Connors or Bjorn Borg, or against John McEnroe, who defeated some of the world's best players before he had reached the age of 21?

It is far easier to single out the game's greatest women. These are without doubt Suzanne Lenglen, the fabulous French star, Helen Wills Moody, who never lost a set between 1927 and 1933, and Maureen Connolly, "Little Mo", whose career was tragically ended when she broke her leg in a riding accident.

Billie Jean King, who has won more Wimbledon championships than any other competitor in the history of the tournament, Virginia Wade, Chris Lloyd and Martina Navratilova are among the great women stars who have thrilled spectators around the world with their brilliant tennis skills.

THEY CAPTURED THE WEST

The hunting party was led by W. F. Cody, a man whose name was to become legendary. At his side rode a young Englishman, Arthur Boyd Houghton, whose task was to produce a true picture of life in the West.

T he hunting party had ridden out from Fort McPherson a few days before and was heading for the tall-grass country between the Platte and Republican rivers. The riders were looking for buffalo. The party consisted of a unit of the Fifth Cavalry and a newcomer to the West, a young English Pre-Raphaelite painter, Arthur Boyd Houghton. The guide was William Frederick Cody, better known throughout that continent as Buffalo Bill.

BECOMING A LEGEND

Cody, at this time, was chief of scouts attached to the Fifth Cavalry at Fort McPherson, Nebraska Territory, and, although only twenty-four years old, his name was already becoming legend. Just two months previously, on December 23rd, 1869, the first instalment of Ned Buntline's "Buffalo Bill, the King of the Border Men" had appeared in the "New York Weekly". He was an impressive figure, this Buffalo Bill Cody. Over 1.90 m tall, with long hair falling over the shoulders of his buckskin jacket from under the wide brim of his sombrero, he looked every inch the Western Hero. No artist "out West" to picture the rugged individualists of the frontier could ask for a better or more picturesque guide. Certainly no white man knew more about hunting buffalo.

Arthur Boyd Houghton was a pictorial journalist, what was known in those days as a Special Artist. This was a new breed of men created by the new pictorial weekly magazines such as the "Illustrated London News" and the "Graphic", who were sent out to foreign lands to bring back pictures. Houghton had been sent by the English magazine, "Graphic", to make a pictorial record of the American West. English readers of that time could have had little idea of what the West was truly like. What impression they did have would probably have derived from the novels of James Fenimore Cooper and Henry Wadsworth Longfellow's "Hiawatha". As such literature portrayed a frontier that had long since disappeared, Houghton's mission was long overdue.

Travelling by the Union Pacific Railroad, Houghton had arrived in

When the long day's trek was over, the hunters relaxed around the campfire. Often the men held impromptu jamborees—and Houghton was there to sketch the scene.

North Platte, Nebraska, and it was here that he met Bill Cody and arranged for the scout to take him buffalo hunting.

During that winter of 1869—70 there was peace on the Northern plains and so the army had decided to come along too! In those days no-one could resist chasing after buffalo, and the men stationed at Fort McPherson were no exception. So it was that Houghton and Cody were joined by a unit of cavalrymen.

ON GUARD

It was shortly after they had passed Red Willow Creek that the party sighted their first buffalo. As well as making a drawing of this moment, Houghton enthusiastically wrote in his notes: "There stands the monster, stock still, gazing at them with the strong, majestic gaze of his tribe. He is the forerunner, outpost, picket of his particular herd, browsing and keeping guard on the frontier of their domain. A great, tough-ribbed, hard and hairy-headed and bearded bull, he is one of that outer circle of buffalo which is always found among the cows and the young. He watches for two

enemies—for the white or Kiota wolf, a cruel, rapacious beast, which stealthily pounces upon their young, their feeble, or their wounded; and for man, in the shape of Indians."

But it wasn't man in the shape of Indians who was the buffalo's enemy this time, and one can imagine the fierce joy on the faces of scout, painter and cavalrymen alike as they galloped after the herd, rifles at the ready.

On returning from the hunt, the party made camp among some cottonwoods along the Platte River. Here they feasted on freshly-killed, roast buffalo steaks, told tall tales of adventure round the campfire and held impromptu dances or "jamborees", as they called them. Houghton did a drawing of this campfire dance, showing the party prancing to the musical drumming of a frying pan beaten by a pistol butt. He also made a drawing of Buffalo Bill—the "captain" of the expedition—watching over his charges.

Another legendary Western scout, and a great friend of Buffalo Bill Cody, was Texas Jack Omohundro. And it was Texas Jack who guided yet another young English Special Artist on his mission to depict the American

West—Valentine Walter Bromley.

In the high summer of 1874 a stage-coach rattled aross the plains carrying a strange assortment of passengers. Inside the swaying Concord sat the plainsman, Texas Jack; the artist, Valentine Walter Bromley; the Earl of Dunraven; the Earl's personal physician, Doctor Kingsley; the Earl's servant, Campbell; the Earl's negro cook and valet, Maxwell; and the Earl's collie dog, "Tweed"! The stage with its odd cargo rattled on north-wards towards Virginia City, Montana Territory.

As Bromley stepped out of the stage at Virginia City, he looked up to see an Indian warrior on horseback, armed to the teeth with a bow and a quiver full of arrows, a silver-mounted revolver, and a Winchester rifle, gazing contemptuously down at him and his fellow passengers. The travellers, in their top hats and frock-coats, must have indeed looked pretty silly to that Bannock brave—as to the majority of the white popula-tion of that little frontier town. Bromley did a watercolour painting of this scene which he entitled "The Noble Savage in Town".

But it was at the Crow Indian Agency on the Mission River where Bromley did his most important pic-tures, depicting domestic Indian life with rare insight and integrity. The first thing Bromley saw as he rode into the Agency through the gateway in the high stockade was some Crow Indians unloading pelts for trade outside a hide-trader's hut. This scene became the first of Bromley's pictures of the Crow Indians and was published in the "Illustrated London News".

CHIEF'S SHIELD

Bromley found the Crow en-campment utterly fascinating. The tepees were formed in a large circle and each one held from twelve to twenty people. Outside the entrance to one tepee was a spear from which hung the chief's shield and his medicine bag. This reminded Brom-ley of the mediaeval knights who also displayed their shields and banners in front of their tents.

Bromley loved to sketch the Crow Indians themselves: the women with their graceful movements and dresses of beautifully-tanned deerskin decor-ated with designs of great intricacy and glowing colour; the tall, splendid-looking warriors with their magnifi-cently long, thick hair which they looked after with the utmost care. Bromley understood why the Crows were known as the dandies of the plains.

One splendid watercolour by Bromley tells us more about the Crow Indian and his attitude towards life than any amount of words. It portrays a chief reclining at his ease, smoking his pipe, whilst one of his wives attends to the braiding of his hair. Bromley called the picture, "The Big Chief's Toilet".

Much of the work of the Special Artist lost a great deal in repro-duction. In those days there were no photomechanical means of reproduc-tion and the drawings were copied by an engraver on to a wood block. Thus the drawing lost spontaneity and freshness when finally presented in the magazine. But, despite such technical drawbacks, such Special Artists as Arthur Boyd Houghton and Valentine Walter Bromley managed to convey to their public back home in England something of the wonder and grandeur of the Western Frontier.

Riding through the gateway into the Agency, Bromley saw some Indians unloading furs which they had come to trade. It became the subject of his first picture of the Crow Indians.

King Of The Ring

John L. Suilivan, the Boston Strong Boy, was one of the most colourful and popular characters boxing has ever known. Although his claim to Champion of the World was never strictly true, he was without doubt the best in the world during his prime, both in the bare-knuckle days and as the first American champion to fight in gloves.

Sullivan won the American Heavyweight Championship when he was twenty-four years old. He took nine rounds, just ten and a half minutes, to K.O. Irish-born Paddy Ryan in February, 1882. Sullivan claimed this victory made him World Champion on form. At that time Jem Mace, the British Champion, was semi-retired. Sullivan fought Mace's successor, Mitchell, twice. The first fight was stopped by the police when Sullivan was winning, and the second contest was declared a draw.

Sullivan had no real cause for complaint, for it was estimated that such tours earned him a million dollars. His last fight under the old bare-knuckle rules was against Jake Kilrain. This was a gruelling affair, beginning at dawn on a sweltering July day in 1889. The fight was held in Missouri. The battle lasted for two and a quarter hours, seventy-five rounds in which hard-hitting, fast-moving Sullivan broke his opponent's ribs.

After his win against Ryan, John L. set out on one of his many tours. He offered $1,000 to any man who could stand against him for three rounds. Only one man ever took that prize. He was a second-rate British heavyweight, Tug Wilson, who cunningly took a count of nine every time he was touched. The trick made Sullivan mad, but it made Wilson a quick fortune.

John L's generosity made him as famous as his fists. He never refused a plea for a loan or a gift of money, be it from a genuine religious charity or a bar-room scrounger. Wherever he went crowds followed, some cheering him out of true admiration, others hoping to get near enough to beg a twenty dollar bill.

His fame and popularity travelled with him when he crossed the Atlantic. On a visit to Victorian London so many people clambered into his hansom cab to shake his hand that the floor collapsed. For a long while afterwards the lucky ones invited others to "Shake the hand that shook the hand of John L. Sullivan".

At the height of his popularity he was presented with a golden belt studded with 400 diamonds, but these were sold, stolen or pawned and the money wasted away with the rest of his earnings. He lost the championship finally to Jim Corbett, who knocked him out in 21 rounds. In later years he married and lived to the age of sixty.

THE MYSTERY OF GRIMES GRAVES

For centuries the mystery of Grime's Graves has baffled people. These large cup-shaped depressions in the ground which are in the south-west corner of Norfolk are not even burial places. The Anglo-Saxons named them "Grime's Graves," the word "graves" meaning to them simply a number of hollows.

Situated on the gentle slope of a dry valley, close to The Breckland, a forest plantation, the "Holes", as an early document calls them, were there even before the time of the Anglo-Saxons. These superstitious people thought their war god, Woden, was making the holes with blows from his thunderbolts. In mediaeval times, Grime's Graves were within the so-called "Hundred of Grimshoe," and it is thought that the Court of the Hundred met at the Graves themselves.

In the 17th century, investigators brought a rather more scientific attitude to bear on the problem. They interpreted the depressions as part of a military camp. In 1739, the Reverend Francis Blomefield wrote about this strange phenomenon in his *History of Norfolk*.

The clergyman was convinced that Grime's Graves were "a curious Danish encampment". He described

A clergyman discovers a pair of antlers during a "dig".

the area as being "in a semi-circular form, consisting of about twelve acres, on the side of a hill, or rising ground, of marl or chalk. In this space are a great number of large pits, joined in a regular manner, one near to another . . . the largest seeming to be in the centre, where possibly the general's or commander's tent was". The author went on to say that a whole army could be contained within the hollows.

Some years later, in 1852, two local parsons, the Rev. C. R. Manning and the Rev. S. T. Pettigrew, decided to dig down to discover if anything lay below the hollows. It was generally accepted by this time that the holes had been made by man, not nature. But what kind or manner of man or men? This still remained a mystery. The two clergymen, like others before them, thought they had discovered the truth, when after digging down just a little way, they found flint debris.

"This is the remains of a paved floor," they thought immediately, and to them a floor meant a home. They concluded that the place was a British town—"a fortified settlement of the Iceni". But Canon W. Greenwell began a new "dig" in 1870 and, after three years of work, his patience was rewarded.

The hollow he was working on was in the south-eastern edge of the area. He found it was in fact a filled-in circular shaft, the shaft of a flint mine.

Digging deeper, the Canon came upon the tools the early men had used, antlers of Red Deer, which acted as picks, and the bones of aurochs (extinct wild oxen of Europe), used for scraping away the sand and chalk, so that the flint could be reached. It was estimated that 50,000 antlers were used at Grime's Graves.

It was an exciting discovery but was it the whole truth? Forty years later the presumed date when the flint mines were worked was challenged by a Mr. R. A. Smith. He held that the mines had been worked even earlier than 3,000 years ago, and digging started up again. From 1914 until 1939, they kept on coming, diggers both professional and amateur, with

The "flint-knappers" were skilled men who shaped the flints into tools.

The Stone Age men hunted Red Deer in the forests because they needed their antlers as tools.

implements in hand to Grime's Graves, to try to work out what these marks were which had been left behind as legacies of the past.

Diggers discovered gallery after gallery radiating from the sunken shafts, and many objects came to light. In 1939, a new and surprising discovery was made—a chalk figure of a goddess on a pedestal with offerings of antlers laid at her feet. There were also further finds of Red Deer images engraved on flint, and chunks of chalk hollowed out and filled with fat into which had been set rough wicks, to light the workers at their tasks. These were the very first miners' lamps.

Modern science suggests that the pits were worked between 2208 B.C.

and 1908 B.C. By measuring the amount of radio-activity left in carbon, it can be judged how old the carbon is, and therefore how old the material is of which the carbon forms a part.

The miners were shrewd men. They hunted the Red Deer in the forests round about, first because they needed their antlers for making tools, but also the skins of the animals were cured and made into thongs which were woven into ladders for the miners to descend into the deep shafts.

But who actually mined Grime's Graves we still do not know. Were there "professional" miners in those days? Or did whole families make a practice of going there in certain seasons? It is thought that the surface workers, the

"knappers," the shapers of flint tools, were skilled professionals. The tools were needed to cut down trees to prepare land for cultivation, also as hunt weapons.

The site of Grime's Graves is the most spectacular group of flint-workings in Britain. Even to this day in the nearby town of Brandon, there is a flint-knapping industry and a village inn called "The Flint-Knappers' Arms".

Everything seems to point to the work of Stone Age men but the question arises, do we really know that this is the final answer to the whole mystery of Grime's Graves? Or will another century prove us just as wrong about the hollows in the hills as were the earlier explorers and archaeologists?

SINGLE SUCCESS

Everyone, says an adage, has one good book in him. It is a saying that sustains many a hopeful new novelist as he toils with paper and pen, only to find, at the end of it all, that the adage is rarely true.

But for Richard Doddridge Blackmore it *was* true. All his life Blackmore toiled with pen and paper, writing novels. Only one of them is remembered, and but for that one, Blackmore's name would be almost unknown in Britain today.

The one book that made Blackmore famous was, of course, the delightful Exmoor romance *Lorna Doone.* Generations of young people have thrilled to the deeds of the wicked outlaw Doones, and have sighed over the lovely Lorna and her romance with John Ridd, the enemy of the Doones.

Critics, who gave Blackmore a hard time with most of his books, have rightly observed that Lorna succeeds as a heroine because she embodies one of Blackmore's basic faults as a writer—an inability to describe people so that they seem to be real. But Lorna needs no description; her beauty is something the reader must see in his mind's eye—and inevitably, helped by Blackmore's melodious prose, he sees her as perfectly beautiful.

In *Lorna Doone* Blackmore attained heights he never reached before or after the book, despite much trying.

Blackmore's father was a country parson, whose wife died while Richard was still a baby. Richard went to Blundell's School in Tiverton, Devon, and thence to Oxford University. After coming down from the university he married and worked first as a lawyer and then as a schoolmaster.

The school holidays gave the young master time to indulge his passion for writing. First came a book of verses, then some Latin translations. With a handsome legacy from an uncle, which assured his future, he became a "gentleman market gardener, and it was as such that his first novel, *Clara Vaughan,* was published.

Clara Vaughan was a manuscript upon which Blackmore had been working off and on for a number of years. It has an imper-

fect plot and was far from successful.

Undeterred, Blackmore continued to tend the fruit trees in his Teddington, Surrey, market garden, and in due time wrote a second novel, called *Cradock Nowell,* which was also a literary failure. It was now plain that while Blackmore could draw brilliant pictures in words of Nature in its serenity and its violence, he was dreadfully uneasy when describing people. His digressions,

too, were so long-winded that when they were finished the poor reader could be forgiven for forgetting what the book was about.

All this was to be changed in one spell-binding flash of inspiration. One day Blackmore read a magazine story called "The Doones of Exmoor" while on a Devon holiday. It must have recalled memories of his childhood in the West Country and awakened a stir of excitement in the shy, dour author, for he noted the story and when he returned home from his holiday he wrote *Lorna Doone*.

When Blackmore presented his manuscript to the publishers they were not very impressed. They printed 500 copies—a small enough order—in the usual three volumes common to Victorian book publishing. But the critics liked it, and the book became a success.

That success was never again to be equalled. Although *Lorna* soon made Blackmore famous, the critical Victorian reading public were unimpressed, and rightly so, by his next novel, *The Maid of Sker*. It was a poor book, full of improbabilities.

Blackmore was now as famous as any literary man in Victorian times. Visiting Americans came to his Teddington house just to

BLACKMORE'S HEROINE

Just as *Lorna Doone* stands out as Blackmore's one great work, so do its principal characters, Lorna Doone and her sweetheart John Ridd, stand out as the only truly remembered creations of their author.

Lorna, daughter of a villainous outlaw family, is every young man's dream of a perfect girl. She it was who stole the heart of sturdy John Ridd, and when she was absent from their regular secret meeting place in springtime, the sorrowing John lamented,

"All the beauty of the spring went for happy men to think of; all the increase of the year was for other eyes to mark. Not a sign of any sunrise for me, from my fount of life; not a breath to stir the dead leaves fallen on my heart's Spring."

After *Lorna Doone* Blackmore persisted in making heroines the chief characters of his stories, whereas in fact his men are always more real. The best of them are undoubtedly Sergeant Jakes and Parson Penniloe of *Perlycross*, a village tale which is well worth reading.

BLACKMORE'S BOOKS

R. D. Blackmore wrote 13 novels. *Lorna Doone,* which passed into more than 40 editions, put him in the front rank of Victorian writers. If he had not written it, two others of his country novels, *Perlycross* and *Mary Anerley,* would have given him a place in the second rank. Another book, *Cripps the Carrier,* is also worth reading for its excellent descriptive passages.

Blackmore's novels, in order of writing, are *Clara Vaughan, Cradock Nowell, Lorna Doone, The Maid of Sker, Alice Lorraine, Cripps the Carrier, Erema, Mary Anerley, Christowell, The Remarkable History of Sir Thomas Upmore, Bart., Springhaven, Kit and Kitty* and *Perlycross.*

get a glimpse of the great author. But all this fame and admiration rested on *Lorna Doone*. His writing output was slowed down, too, by the increasing demands of his orchards on his time as a result of crop failure, and by illness.

Blackmore touched for a moment some of his former greatness with a new novel, *Perlycross*. "When shall we have another *Lorna Doone?"* clamoured the critics. Yielding to pressure, Blackmore wrote a book containing four short stories, one of which brought the Doones briefly back to life. The story, however, proved conclusively that the master touch was gone, a fact he must have realised before his death in the first month of the twentieth century.

THE CREW THAT RETURNED FROM THE DEAD

For more than four years, the steamship *Victory* was the only home that Captain John Ross and his crew knew.

In the spring of 1828, Ross had led an expedition from England to explore the regions near the North Pole. The men had not intended to stay away so long, but when the *Victory* became icebound, they were forced into a "frightful imprisonment."

Unable to communicate with the outside world, Ross patiently waited for the ice to melt. But as the months went by and this showed no signs of happening, he realised that something drastic must be done.

Although he did not know it, he and his crew had already been given up for dead; at home in Britain, the men's families were in mourning, and there was no move to send out any rescue vessels.

On 29th May, 1832, Captain Ross decided to abandon ship. He and his crew did this with mixed feelings, for although they were glad to be leaving the ice, they had regrets about deserting the *Victory*.

The ship's colours were hoisted and nailed to the mast, and a final toast was drunk. Then the crew of the *Victory* started out on one of the most arduous journeys in the history of Polar exploration—and certainly one with a most unexpected ending.

It took the party a month to reach a place called Fury Beach, where they built a rough timber house and began to repair the three boats which they had left there earlier. They also dug out the food which they had wisely hidden in the snow. Thus the threat of starvation was removed, at least for the time being.

Ross proposed to sail to the Barrow Strait in Canada, and then continue across the Arctic Circle, south to civilization. The ice was now beginning to break at Fury Beach, and after taking aboard enough provisions for two months, the mariners set off.

They sailed night and day until at last, in the middle of September, they came to the meeting point of Barrow Strait and Prince Regent's Inlet. Here, to their bitter disappointment, their way was barred by a continuous mass of solid ice. Unable to make any

118

For four back-breaking hours they pursued the vessel, until she was no more than a dot on the horizon.

further progress, they were forced to return to Fury Beach to sit out yet another winter in the frozen wilderness.

The following months had a disastrous effect on the men's morale. The long hours of boredom and inactivity made them ill-tempered and morose. Their supply of food began to run short, and they were further depressed by the death of the carpenter, one of the most valued members of the crew.

Somehow Ross managed to keep their hopes alive until July, when they made another attempt to escape from their "dismal prison." Three of the seamen were now so seriously ill that they were unable to walk. Some of the others were not much stronger, and it was all the castaways could do to pull the loaded sledges to the spot on the beach where they had left the boats.

"We prepared to quit this dreary place," wrote Ross, "as we hoped, for ever. Yet with these hopes there were mingled many fears . . . whether we might not yet be compelled to return—to return once more to despair, and perhaps to return to die."

By 12th July, they had safely reached the boats. They spent the next few days cutting a lane through the ice, and at eight o'clock on the third morning they joyfully set sail. The sick men were laid gently in the bottom of the boats and, fired with new enthusiasm, the fit seamen rowed for three days and nights, until a fierce snowstorm forced them to land and pitch their tents.

Next morning, they again set sail. The lane of open water they were following through the ice was now broadening before them, and this gave them heart.

For a number of days they struggled on, always keeping close to the shore so that at nights they could land and take shelter.

Then, one morning, while they were still ashore, the look-out spotted a sail in the distance. Immediately the boats were launched, and in a dead calm the oarsmen pulled lustily towards the vessel.

The party's hopes of rescue were, however, quickly dashed. A breeze suddenly sprang up, the ship's sails filled, and she headed rapidly away from them. Even so, Ross and his companions did not despair. For four back-breaking hours they pursued the ship until she was eventually no more than a dot on the horizon.

For a while, it seemed as if their situation was as lamentable as ever. Then, miraculously, a second sail was sighted. The men from the *Victory* had come across a whaling fleet.

This time they were confident of being picked up, and, sure enough, as it again fell calm, a boat was lowered from the whaler and headed towards the overjoyed crew.

As it came within hailing distance, an extraordinary conversation took place between Captain Ross and the officer in command of the longboat.

"Have you lost your ship?" called out the officer.

"Yes," answered Ross. "What is your vessel's name?"

"The *Isabella*, whaler, of Hull—commanded by Captain Humphreys."

Ross's heart jumped in his chest. "And formerly commanded by Captain Ross?" he called back.

"That's right. But Ross has been dead these two years."

"No he hasn't," replied Ross stoutly. "I'm Ross, and the *Isabella* used to be *my* ship!"

Once the officer had got over his amazement, he had the exhausted survivors transferred to the long-boat and taken aboard the *Isabella*, where Ross was given three rousing cheers by the crew.

At first, Ross was ill at ease at being back on his old ship. Unshaven, dirty, and "dressed in the rags of wild beasts," both he and his crew were sensitive about their "gaunt and grim" looks. But by the time they reached England, they were ready and willing to meet anyone.

The story of how they had come back from the dead was one of the most remarkable in the history of the Arctic.

FIGHT FOR SURVIVAL

The word "cuddly" might have been especially invented for the koala bear, which is not, as it happens, a bear at all! To add to the confusion, it is the only "bear" which looks remotely like the ever-popular "Teddy bear," named in honour of the American President Theodore Roosevelt, who was a mighty hunter and wiper-out of animals.

Koalas are natives of Australia. They are climbing marsupials and are quite harmless and very popular with humans. If really provoked they have been known to scratch, though there are few records of this happening.

A young koala is born in an undeveloped state after a gestation period of 25 days. It is then carried in its mother's pouch for a further six months before it emerges to cling to her back for another period of six months.

The koala would be a tremendous draw in any zoo, outshining all rivals, but, unfortunately for humans, it cannot be kept in captivity on account of its highly specialised diet of eucalyptus leaves, and only certain types of eucalyptus leaves at that. The leaves of some species of eucalyptus contain deadly poison, such as prussic acid, at certain seasons.

The koala has to know which leaves are edible and when. Outside Australia it is impossible to keep koalas. Even if eucalyptus trees were imported, it does not follow that the change of soil and climate would produce suitable food.

Today, these delightful animals are safe, but they were only made so at the last moment. They were all too easy to hunt and were almost wiped off the face of the Earth. The reason was the koala's thick, wooly pelt, which was highly marketable, added to which so-called sportmen were doing their worst.

Being a slow breeder, the koala could not keep pace with the toll taken by hunters, and in Australia there is always the danger of a bush fire. These two reasons, plus disease, make it a miracle that any survived.

MADE UP FOR THE PAST

Fortunately, since the end of the Second World War Australian wildlife departments have made up for the behaviour of officials and private citizens in the past. From an all-time low of 10,000 koalas, there are now more than 40,000 of them in the State of Victoria alone. It is a happy ending to an unpleasant story.

Another animal which resembles a bear but may not be one is the giant panda. Arguments rage among zoologists as to whether this famous creature is a small bear or a giant racoon. Whatever the answer is finally proved to be, the animal is on the danger list of animals facing extinction.

Strangely, though the giant panda is on the danger list, not everyone agrees that it should be. It is an uncommon animal, found mainly in the mountainous forests of western Szechwan in west China, but it is now though that its range is far wider than anyone imagined, taking in Tibet, Kansu in the north, and Yunnan in the south.

Another fortunate factor is that the Chinese think very highly of the giant panda and do their very best to protect it. As for the inhabitants of Szechwan, one trembles to think what they would do to any outsider who dared to molest the great animal of which they are so justifiably proud.

The Chinese have even managed to

The Chinese have a high regard for the panda and make every effort to protect it.

Right: A magnificent markhor, a wild Asian goat in danger of extinction. Below: The popular koala bear, which is not a bear at all! It was saved from being wiped out at the very last moment. Because of its feeding habits, only the Australians can enjoy its company.

mate pandas in the Peking Zoo, which is more than the London and Moscow zoos succeeded in doing with their famous captives, An-An and Chi-Chi. Several pandas have been born in Peking Zoo.

As for the general public, they have given the giant panda the final accolade of popularity—that of turning it into a fluffy toy.

There are many lesser-known animals in danger of extinction. The markhor, a species of wild goat which ranges the mountains on the borders of Afghanistan, Kashmir and the USSR is one such animal.

Fortunately, only the jerdoni, the straight-horned markhor which ranges the Baluchistan-Afghanistan border, is considered to be faced with immediate extinction. Little is known about the animal, except that hunters and poachers are after it and, so the story goes, troops have been known to mow down herds with automatic weapons.

All types of markhor have magnificent horns which are greatly twisted. As the picture shows, they are superb animals, in keeping with the wild, mountainous country they inhabit. Little is known about the markhor's way of life because of the desolate places it inhabits.

Yet however desolate an area an animal ranges, hunters and poachers will find it out. At last the danger is being fully realised by an ever-growing number of people, just as it is realised that pollution can choke the rivers and seas. A species of mammal gets wiped out every year and, once gone, it can never be replaced. Organisations like the World Wildlife Fund fight to change the situtation. The public is becoming aware of the dangers facing many animals.

Conservation of nature, including its animals, is at last having some effect. Incredibly, people who used to recommend it were sometimes regarded as freaks! Yet even now the sheer extent of the danger is hard to grasp. About 1,000 kinds of vertebrate animals—creatures with backbones—are threatened with extinction. No wonder international and national preservation societies are striving to get home the message that without action there will be no wildlife left.

MARATHON MEN

The Marathon is the oldest race in the world, and is the only foot race of international status that is known by its name rather than its length. In fact, most people would be hard put to name its exact length. Since 1924, the Olympic Marathon has been 25 miles 385 yards long. Because it is run in varying conditions and over different terrain, there can be no real world record for the race which has given its name to many other feats of endurance.

The Marathon has its origin in a battle fought in 490 B.C., when a drastically outnumbered army of Greeks faced a vast horde of invading Persians on the Plain of Marathon some 35 kilometres from Athens. Miltiades, the Greek general, won a brilliant victory over the invaders and drove them back to their ships.

The battle over, Pheidippides was ordered to carry the triumphant news to the anxious citizens of Athens. He ran all the way to the city at full speed. On arrival he shouted, "Rejoice! We conquer!" Then he collapsed and died from exhaustion.

During the ancient Olympic Games, the Marathon was one of the main events held in honour of the great runner, Pheidippides. The victor's prize was a wreath of sacred laurel. When the modern Olympics were inaugurated in Athens in 1896, the Marathon again became one of the main races, and the first modern Olympic Marathon was won by a Greek, Spyridou Louis.

In the 1907 Olympics, the Italian, Dorando Pietri, collapsed several times as he struggled towards the finishing line in the White City Stadium, London. Out of pity, officials helped him across the line. He was the first to cross, but was disqualified for receiving help. Such was his heroism and disappointment, that Queen Alexandra gave him a special gold cup as a consolation prize.

A similar fate befell the British champion, Jim Peters, in the British Empire and Commonwealth games in Vancouver in 1954. He collapsed from heat and exhaustion within sight of the tape. His courage earned him a special award from the Duke of Edinburgh.

There has been unexpected triumph too, as when Emil Zatopec, who had already won the 5,000 and 10,000 metres in the 1952 Olympics at Helsinki, suddenly decided to run in the Marathon for the first time in his life. He won! The toughest test of all is the annual South African Comrades (double) Marathon run between Durban and Pietermaritzburg, a distance of over 86 kilometres. One of the most consistent Marathon runners in modern times is the Ethiopian Abebe Bikila, who won barefoot in 1960 to beat Zatopec's record.

THE CASTLE ON THE HILLTOP

If ghosts exist then Maiden Castle must be a haunted spot. There were men there 5,000 years ago, long before the people we call the Ancient Britons. Its old name conjures up its air of mystery far better than its modern one. It is Mai Dun.

Mai Dun is near Dorchester in Dorset, the town which was once the Roman town of Durnovaria. "Maiden Castle" suggests something mediaeval, but there is nothing of the Middle Ages about the place. It is sometimes called a "hill-fort", but even this is inaccurate. It was, in fact, a whole city made impregnable by ridge upon ridge of earthworks. The grass is now green over these ridged defences, and sheep graze over the high table-land.

The writer Thomas Hardy was awed by Mai Dun, and wrote of it as having an almost animal aspect, "an enormous many-limbed organism of antediluvian times . . . lying lifeless and covered with a thin green cloth . . ."

Something of the story of the many peoples who made and lived in the fortress was revealed when the site was excavated between 1934 and 1937 by the archaeologist Sir Mortimer Wheeler.

It was discovered that three quite different communities had lived on the hilltop and fashioned its outlines. First were Late Stone Age men, who built their village of 10 to 15 acres on the eastern part of the later city.

These people made flat-bottomed ditches, and left behind them flint axes, tools of bone and horn, and handmade pottery. They also left a chalk idol, crudely carved, but shaped well enough for us to see that it was of an Earth Goddess. Just why these early men left their village we do not know. The hilltop was deserted.

Then Mai Dun became a burial place. From knoll to knoll and across the filled-in ditches a mound was built, in all about 550 metres long. This "Bank-Barrow" is perhaps the largest of its type in Britain. Most of it was destroyed by the builders of the later city, but in the earth they left a very grisly skeleton.

It was of a man of about 30, 1.6 metres tall. Immediately after his death he had been hacked to pieces, and an attempt to get at his brain by a circular incision in the skull had been made. Perhaps there may have been a ritual eating of the brain to absorb the dead man's virtues; perhaps it was an early attempt at surgery.

Later, a new people wandered westwards from the Low Countries and settled for a while at Mai Dun. These "Beaker People", so-called for their distinctive pottery, did not remain long, and for many cen-

Iron Age people settled Mai Dun hill about the year 250 B.C., building a village on the site of an old one.

turies the heights were deserted. Scrub grew over the remains of the villages and the Bank-Barrow. A solitary Bronze Age spear of the period has been found, which was probably owned by a lone hunter.

Next, Iron Age people settled all over Britain, bringing a new culture and new ways of farming, but it was not until about 250 B.C. that families of these folk climbed the hill and settled on the old village site. They made wall-like ramparts, first with timber, then with thin limestone slabs quarried locally.

Safely enclosed, they built timber huts, storage pits and streets. They grew corn on small, square fields, and ground it on stone slabs. Cloth was also woven. Chalk was used for loom-weights, and the people had weaving combs.

Slowly, the village prospered, finally covering 45 acres. The settlement always had two entrances, east and west, and now that it was a town, these entrances were screened by double gateways, with the whole protected by a single rampart and a ditch.

SEAFARERS

War had hardly touched the township, but new men did arrive at Mai Dun as refugees from wars. These were a tribe called the Veneti, sea-faring people from South Brittany who had traded with Cornwall for years and probably married local girls. Cornwall and Brittany have the same "Cliff Castles," and the sling was a weapon common to both peoples.

In 56 B.C., the Veneti, bearing in mind their sea-trade, went to help the northern Gauls against Caesar, but after a brisk naval action off the Breton coast, they were defeated by the Romans. Every member of the Veneti's Senate was killed, and every captive sold into slavery. Some of those who escaped fled to Mai Dun and took command of it.

The Veneti brilliantly remodelled the hilltop city with a maze of banks and ditches. They built stone platforms at vantage points for sling-throwers to defend the approaches. They flanked the gateways with high limestone walls, and they brought a more advanced way of life to Mai Dun.

They left evidence of this in their bead-rimmed pottery and in their great hoards of sling-stones. One hoard contained 20,000 stones, probably beach-stones collected from the Chesil Beach.

Seventy-five years later, the powerful Belgae arrived. The new settlers reconstructed streets,

The Romans stormed Mai Dun in A.D. 44, but not before they had suffered heavy casualties from the slingstones rained down on them by the defenders. Later, the few survivors left Mai Dun for Dorchester.

and their upturned shields, the Romans hacked their way through the maze of fortifications and entered the settlement itself.

What followed was brief, bloody and complete, with women and children perishing was well as men. Vespasian, having taught the inhabitants a sharp lesson about the power of Rome, left the few survivors to bury their dead.

DEADLY ARROWS

Excavations have revealed arrows among the outer works and, among the buried, one man with an arrow through his vertebra. This earliest British war cemetery reveals not only mass-burials, but also the fact that the survivors found time to bury with their dead food, drink and jewellery.

It was the end of Maiden Castle: within 20 years its last survivors had moved to Roman Durnovaria. The hill returned to nature.

The excavators also found a small temple of a much later date. Four priests were buried nearby. Who built this temple, with its bronze plaque bearing the figure of the Roman goddess Minerva, and the three-horned bull-god of Britain and Gaul? Was this the temple of some Romano-Celtic religion? And who was the warrior with a short sword and knife, buried there around 600, when the temple had long been a ruin? And why was he left in the silence of the once proud city of Maiden Castle—Mai Dun?

Vespasian later became an Emperor of Rome.

abolished grain-pits, replacing them with barns, and further improved the defences. But Rome was on the march, and the Belgae had little time to enjoy their settlement in peace.

Around A.D. 44 Vespasian, later to become an Emperor, set out with the 2nd Augustan Legion to subdue south-west Britain. Among the 20 townships he had to deal with was Mai Dun. Soon the legion was approaching the seven-fold ramparts of the great hill.

The tough legionaries were greeted with such a hail of sling-stones that they had to retreat and reform. The Romans then replied with a storm of high-flying arrows, many of them fire-tipped. These ignited some huts just inside the fort, and, under cover of smoke

The Romans defeated the Veneti of South Brittany at sea in 56 B.C. Later, some of the Veneti fled across the Channel and settled at Mai Dun.

The nightmare began on the night of the 29th November, 1942, and a hundred people will remember that date until their dying day, which at the time seemed very close.

The British liner, *Dunedin Star,* had that night struck an unknown object off the coast of South West Africa. The vessel was bound for the Middle East with a valuable cargo of troop supplies.

Her commander, Captain R. B. Lee, realised that the ship was doomed. So in an endeavour to save the hundred people aboard, he headed towards the grim, unwelcoming coastline of South West Africa, which has been called "The Coast of Death".

Just before midnight, the liner ran aground. A motor-boat took a party of sixty-three people to the beach, including women and children. The majority of the crew remained on the ship.

On reaching the beach, the survivors made a camp for themselves in the sand-dunes and used the sails from an abandoned lifeboat to erect a shelter for the women and children.

Shortly the castaways were suffering agonies from sores caused by sunburn, and from fierce sandstorms which lashed their faces and bodies. They were also in desperate need of food and drink, but the vicious breakers prevented help from the stranded liner from reaching them.

An attempt to reach them was made, this time by air. On December 3rd, a bomber flown by Captain Immins Naude, took off from Cape Town on a rescue mission.

SANDSTORM

Unfortunately, the rescue attempt was doomed. Captain Naude, after dropping supplies, brought the bomber down on the beach three kilometres from the makeshift camp. But, as luck would have it, a sandstorm struck the bomber, which became bogged down in the sand. Naude was unable to budge his craft so he and his crew of three had to settle down with the survivors and await the *next* rescue party.

This rescue party composed of troop-carriers had, in fact, already set out from Windhoek, the capital of South West Africa.

As the convoy fought its way towards the coast, the tyres on the trucks became scorched and radiator caps were blown in the air by the force of the overheated water.

At last, a minesweeper, *Nerine,* anchored itself off the beach and fourteen men were literally dragged to safety.

Then on December 12th, the trucks finally churned through the sand to within reach of the camp.

After those of the castaways who were suffering from exposure had been medically treated, the convoy started on the return journey.

Ten days later, at lunchtime, on Christmas Eve, it toiled into Windhoek, where the rescuers and rescued were given a tumultuous reception.

Today, the Coast of Death is as desolate and frightening as ever. Denied the hundred castaways who were snatched from its shore on that occasion, it awaits the next ship unlucky enough to come to grief there.